The Pictorial History of B.O.A.C and Associated Airlines

SCOVAL
PUBLISHING LTD

© 2015 Scott Henderson.

British Library Cataloguing in Publication Data
A catalogue record for this book is available from the British Library

ISBN: 978 1 902236 14 8

Published by:
SCOVAL Publishing Ltd.
PO Box 36
Ponteland
Newcastle-upon-Tyne
NE20 9WE
England
Tel: (01661) 820838

e mail: scovalpublishing@tiscali.co.uk

Printed by Martins The Printers Co Berwick Upon Tweed.

Edited by S Henderson, C Hymers.
Designed by Scott Henderson for SCOVAL Publishing Ltd.

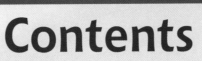

Contents

ACKNOWLEDGMENTS

The author and publisher wish to thank the following people for their help in many ways, in which we are most grateful — Jeff Birch, the late Roger Jackson of the A.J.Jackson Collection, the late John Stroud, Mel Lawrence, Klaus Vomhof, Dr. Mark Nicholes of Cambridge University, the R.A.F. Museum Hendon. Pat Mc Ginnis of Boeing (nee McDonnell Douglas), Long Beach, U.S.A, and Tom Lubesmeyer of Boeing, Seattle, Barry Guess and Mike Fielding of BAE Systems Farnborough, George Jenks of British Aerospace Heritage, Woodford, David Charlton of BAE/Airbus Industries Bristol, James Strong, Dominic Dunne and Laurana Haines of Qantas and Sonja Grünbauer of South African Airways. Special thanks go to Roy James, Nick Webb and Jonathan Taylor.

FOREWORD

Always a subject that I have had a passion for since early school days, whenever possible I would cut out newspaper articles and collect photographs on any subject matter related to BOAC and any Associated Airline connected with the state monolith. Over the years since its demise an idea began to form in my mind that eventually, when I acquired enough information, stickers and photographs, I would attempt to write the complete history of the airline.

During 1995, I was fortunate to acquire a collection of colour slides relating to British and Commonwealth airlines, taken over the years since the late fifties by Peter R Keating, the renowned BOAC chief steward and photographer. Within that collection was a large volume of very rare images of BOAC and Associated Airlines' aircraft taken in exotic locations around the world.

With the formation of Scoval Publishing in 1998, I realised that the possibility of producing the book had materialised and the work began that would take many years of research to produce this history of possibly the most interesting and complex series of airline formations created during the last millennium.

Scott Henderson
Ponteland
Newcastle upon Tyne
2014

B·O·A·C 1940~1945

BOAC inherited nine de Havilland DH.86 Express airliners from Imperial Airways. Two flew the Bangkok-Hong Kong route until October 1940, then operated trans-African services until replaced in October 1941 with Lockheed twins and Junkers JU52/3ms. Imperial Airways DH.86A G-ADUG (c/n 2335) 'Danae' in 1936.

A parliamentary investigation into the efficiency of Imperial Airways Ltd. and British Airways Ltd. (BAL) resulted in the airlines merging on 24th November 1939, establishing a new airline under the name of British Overseas Airways Corporation (BOAC) with Sir John Reith as Chairman and Clive Pearson as Deputy Chairman.

Imperial Airways had been formed, under the chairmanship of Sir Eric Geddes, on 31st March 1924 by the merger of British Marine Air Navigation Co. Ltd, Daimler Airway, Handley Page Transport Ltd. and Instone Air Line Ltd. The airline was the British Government's first 'Chosen Instrument' to operate overseas air services and was awarded a £1 million subsidy to develop air services over the next ten years linking countries of the British Empire.

Allied British Airways Ltd., registered by Whitehall Securities on 30th September 1935, was formed by merging Spartan Air Lines and United Airways. With Clive Pearson as Chairman, it was renamed British Airways (BA) on 29th October 1935 and acquired Hillman Airways in December and British Continental Airways in April 1936. BA was awarded contracts to carry mail to Denmark, Germany, Holland and Sweden, and to operate passenger flights to Scandinavia and Germany.

During 1937, the MP Robert Perkins raised

Saunders-Roe A.19 Cloud G-ABHG (c/n A19/2) 'Flying Amo' was based at Hythe and trained Imperial Airways' flying-boat crews at the School of Basic Marine Instruction in 1939. It was inherited by BOAC in 1940.

B·O·A·C 1940~1945

Two Lockheed 10A Electras G-AEPR (c/n 1083) 'Leith' and G-AFCS (c/n 1025) 'Lea' were inherited from British Airways in April 1940 and were based in Cairo, flying to the Middle East and across Africa. These all-metal aircraft, configured for ten passengers, were powered by two 450hp Pratt and Whitney Wasp Juniors and had a respectable cruising speed of 190mph.
Above: British Airways Electra G-AEPN (c/n 1080) taken in 1937. It was impressed into the RAF in 1939 and operated by No. 24 Squadron at Hendon.
Below: A British Airways' Electra running engines in 1937.

concerns in Parliament over safety issues and the poor treatment of Imperial Airways' pilots. He asked for a public inquiry into British civil aviation which led to the formation of a Committee of Inquiry into Civil Aviation headed by the Rt. Hon. Lord Cadman as Chairman. The Cadman Committee Report was presented to Viscount Swinton, Secretary of State for Air, on 8th February 1938 and recommended that Imperial Airways should concentrate on developing the Empire routes (to Africa, Australia, India and North America), whilst British Airways would further develop the European routes.

On 1st July 1938, Imperial Airways announced that Sir John Reith, former Director-General of the BBC, was to be appointed as Chairman of Imperial Airways. He took over shortly before the British Government announced, on 11th November 1938, the intention to merge Imperial Airways and British Airways Ltd. to form a single 'chosen instrument' - the British Overseas Airways Corporation (BOAC).

The Bill received Royal Assent on 4th August 1939 and BOAC was formally established on 24th November 1939 with Sir John Reith as Chairman and the Hon. Clive Pearson as Deputy Chairman. When Sir John Reith resigned to become Minister of Information, Clive Pearson took over as BOAC Chairman in January 1940.

The two companies started working together immediately, although operations under the BOAC name did not start until 1st April 1940 with a total of sixty-nine aircraft of thirteen different types.

In September 1938 the Prime Minister, Neville Chamberlain, had returned

BOAC inherited five ex-British Airways Lockheed 14-WF62 Super Electras powered by 900hp Wright Cyclone engines. They carried twelve passengers at 228mph over 800 miles. Photo of G-AFGN (c/n 1467), used by Prime Minister Neville Chamberlain to travel to the Munich Conference where he signed the appeasement document 'Peace in our Time' with Adolf Hitler on 30th September 1938.

home from a meeting with Hitler in Munich declaring "peace in our time". The following year, however, German Forces invaded Bohemia on 14th March and Hitler announced that Czechoslovakia ceased to exist. German Forces then invaded Poland on the 1st September 1939 which led to Britain and France declaring war on Germany on 3rd September 1939.

Following the formal declaration of war by the British Government, all civil flying ceased and BOAC would spend the next 6 years supporting military operations. Imperial Airways and British Airways moved their separate headquarters from London to a joint BOAC Headquarters in the Clifton Grand Spa Hotel, Bristol, whilst their landplane maintenance facilities were moved away from the London Airports of Croydon and Heston to Whitchurch in Bristol, and the BOAC flying-boats were moved from Southampton to Poole in Dorset and to Durban in South Africa.

Sir Francis Shelmerdine, Director-General of Civil Aviation controlled British civil air activities from 2nd

The Curtiss-Wright C.W.20 (c/n101) was fitted with long-range fuel tanks. It flew Leuchars - Stockholm in early 1942 and Gibraltar - Malta from May to October. It was scrapped at Filton, Bristol in 1943. Photo taken at Whitchurch Bristol in 1942.

In 1942 Armstrong Whitworth A.W.38 Whitley V freighters operated Leuchars-Stockholm and Whitchurch-Gibraltar-Malta. From November 1942 to May 1943 they flew Whitchurch-Rineanna. Photo of G-AGCF (Serial BD360).

B·O·A·C 1940~1945

G-AGGY (LT176) in BOAC livery, one of twenty Avro Anson Mk.1s. The aircraft was flown to Egypt in July 1943, believed to be for No. 28 (Transport) Squadron South African Air Force.

Above: ITCA and Imperial A.W.15 Atalantas operated Calcutta-Allahabad-Cawnpore-Delhi-Jodhpur-Karachi in 1940/41. G-ABTL (c/n AW784) was transferred to the Indian Air Force in March 1941 as Serial DG450.

*Below:
Ex-Imperial Airways'
Short-Mayo
Composite aircraft.*

*The top component
is Short S.20
G-ADHJ (c/n S.796)
'Mercury',
originally built with
four 340hp Napier
Rapier V engines.
The lower compo-
nent is Short S.21
G-ADHK (c/n S.797)
'Maia' powered by
four 920hp Bristol
Pegasus XC.*

*'Maia' was convert-
ed to a 'C' class air-
liner in November
1940 and 'Mercury'
went to No. 320 RAF
(Dutch) Squadron.*

Three Boeing 314As were bought from Pan American Airways for the West African service. They were BOAC's largest aircraft in WWII. Photo of G-AGCA (c/n 2082) 'Berwick' which flew Prime Minister Winston Churchill from Norfolk Virginia to Bermuda on 15th January 1942, after attending a conference with President Roosevelt. The following day Churchill continued his flight to Plymouth, a distance of 3,365 miles/5,415 kms in 17hrs 55mins non-stop.

September under the National Air Communications (NAC) at the Air Ministry. All air services from Britain to Europe were suspended, with the exception of the Heston-Paris service which was resurrected on the 11th October, and the Empire flying-boats weekly flights UK-Kisumu, UK-Durban, and twice weekly UK-Sydney. The twice weekly Perth-Stavanger-Oslo-Stockholm service operated by Junkers JU-52/ms and Lockheed 14s also continued, and the Shoreham/Heston-Bordeaux-Marseilles-Tunis-Malta-Sollum-Alexandria route flown by the de Havilland Albatross was extended to Karachi with Handley Page Hannibal aircraft.

Under BOAC, the Ministry of Aircraft Production (MAP) formed a 'Reserve Organisation' of 'A' licence pilots to operate communications services, ferry aircraft for the RAF and Royal Navy, and to fly light communication duties. It was called the Air Transport Auxiliary (ATA) and was formed with the help of Gerrard d'Erlanger, a BOAC Board Member, who became the ATA Commander in Charge (later BOAC Chairman May 1956). This was the nucleus of the Air Transport Auxiliary (ATA), which included eight female pilots in the crew roster, and the head-quarters and maintenance base were established at White Waltham, Maidenhead on 1st January 1940.

BOAC had inherited 69 aircraft of thirteen types with twelve different engines, an insufficient fleet to perform all tasks required. To increase recognition as British civil aircraft and to avoid being shot at by friend

Avro 683 Lancaster Mk.1 (DV379) G-AGJI, flown by BOAC's Development Flight in 1944-1946, was used for testing airborne equipment and Merlin 102 engines for use in the Avro Tudor.

B·O·A·C 1940~1945

The DH.91 Albatross, fitted with four 525hp de Havilland Gipsy 12s, had a 210mph/338kph cruise speed and range of 1,040 miles/1,674 kms. They operated Heston-Alexandria and Heston-Lisbon in 1940, Bristol-Dublin from July 1941 to February 1942, then later Bristol-Rineanna until 16th July 1943 when 'Fortuna' crashed due to the failure of the wooden rear fuselage and the fleet was grounded. Flyimg above is ex-G-AEVW, (c/n 6801) 'Franklin', the mailplane version painted in RAF camouflage colours.

and foe, they were painted with very large registration letters underlined in red, white and blue stripes. The title of 'British Airways' or 'British Overseas Airways' was also applied until later when this was changed to the full British Overseas Airways Corporation name.

During 1940 the aircraft were camouflaged and then, in 1941, the Speedbird insignia was added along with fleet names. BOAC acquired new and second-hand aircraft from the British Air Ministry and American 'Lend-Lease' bomber aircraft which were hurriedly modified to carry passengers and cargo. The airline was fortunate to acquire three Boeing 314As from Pan American World Airways (PAA), as well as several airliners which escaped to England from Denmark, Holland, Norway and Poland (including 6 Douglas aircraft of KLM), and these were promptly leased.

As the war continued, German Forces invaded Denmark and Norway and, on 9th April 1940, the service from Perth, Scotland to Oslo and Stockholm was suspended. The ex-British Airways' Junkers JU 52/3m G-AFAP 'Jason' was captured by the Germans during an attack on Oslo and, in the first week of May, two Short S.30 'C' class flying boats, G-AFCV 'Caribou' and G-AFCU 'Cabot', were bombed at Bodo in Norway. German troops then invaded Holland, Belgium and Luxembourg on the 10th May, followed by France on the 21st May. Following the resignation of Neville Chamberlain, Winston Churchill became Prime Minister and formed a new War Cabinet on 10th/11th May 1940.

Between 26th May and 4th June, the British

G-AFYF (c/n 95006) 'King Alfred', a DH.95 Flamingo, seen at Bramcote, Nuneaton in November 1940. This was de Havilland's first stressed skin all-metal airliner, powered by two 930hp Bristol Perseus XVI engines which gave a cruising speed of 184mph/296kph. BOAC's fleet of eight were based at Asmara in Eritrea from 1941-1943.

BOAC operated various Consolidated Liberator types. G-AGFN (Serial FL 909) was one of six Liberator IIIs used by the airline.

Expeditionary Forces (BEF) in Europe were pushed back to Dunkirk and evacuated, under Operation Dynamo, by sea to England. Two Ensigns were lost during this period - G-ADSZ 'Elysian' at Merville on 22nd May and G-ADSX 'Ettrick' at Le Bourget on 1st June.

On 10th June, Italy entered the war on the side of Germany and soon after France capitulated on 17th June, signing an armistice with Hitler on the 22nd June 1940.

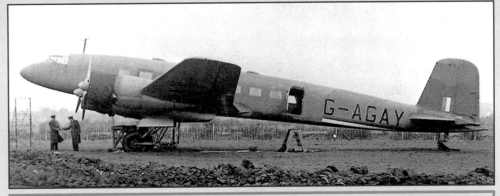

Focke-Wulf Fw200A-02 Condor G-AGAY (c/n 2894) 'Wulf', previously OY-DAM of Danish Airlines D.D.L. (Det Danske Luftfartselskab), was interned on 8th April 1940 at Shoreham. It was registered to BOAC before transfer to the ATA but crashed while landing at White Waltham Airfield Berkshire on the 12th July 1941.

With the trans-Mediterranean route severed between the UK-Egypt and Middle East, BOAC opened a West-African route on 6th August 1940 with Empire boat G-AFCX 'Clyde' from Poole-Lisbon-Bathurst-Freetown-Lagos, connecting with the trans-African service flown by Elders Colonial Airways (ECA) and BOAC.

Three Junkers Ju 52/3ms inherited from British Airways were re-engined with 600hp Pratt and Whitney Wasps: G-AERU (c/n 5440) 'Juno', G-AERX (c/n 5518) 'Jupiter', an ex-A.B. Aerotransport of Sweden aircraft, and also G-AFAP (c/n 5881) 'Jason', a freighter with blanked-off windows. 'Jason' was captured by the Germans at Oslo in April 1940 whilst the others were shipped to Lagos in November 1940 to fly the trans-African route. Both were later sold to SABENA in October 1941 and then chartered to BOAC for the Egypt-Belgium Congo-West Africa service.

B·O·A·C 1940~1945

Lockheed Lodestar (c/n 18-2093) was built as a model 18-07 with Pratt and Whitney Hornet engines. BOAC leased the aircraft from the RAF and fitted 1,200hp Wright Cyclone engines converting it to a model 18-56 with an increased cruise speed of 251mph. G-AGCM 'Lake Mariut' is seen over Cairo in 1942 before being returned to the RAF in August 1946 after the war.
BOAC had a large fleet of Lodestars based at Cairo which flew services into the Western Desert, and to West and East Africa and also the Middle East.

ECA had been founded on 7th November 1935 by Imperial Airways and the Elder-Dempster Shipping Line Ltd. and began services from Lagos-Accra on 11th October 1937. When ECA ceased operations on 14th June 1940 (see Nigerian Airways), BOAC continued the services utilising de Havilland 86 aircraft.

When Italy entered the war on 10th June 1940, the Mediterranean section of the UK-Australia route was severed, stranding 16 BOAC Short 'C' class flying-boats south of Italy at the time. These were then used to open a new 'Horseshoe' route on the 19th June from the Durban base via Cairo to Singapore, with Qantas Short 'C' class flying boats flying from Singapore to Sydney.

TEAL continued the route from Sydney-New Zealand across the Tasman Sea to Auckland (1342mls/2159kms) with two Short S.30 'C' class flying boats named 'Aotearoa' and 'Awarua'. BOAC then reopened the trans-African route on

16th August (Takoradi-Accra-Lagos-Kano-Maiduguri-Fort Lamy-El Geneina-El Fasher-Khartoum-Wadi Halfa-Cairo) using Lockheed 14s on a weekly service and a fortnightly service operated by DH.86s which included stops at Oshogbo, Minna, Kaduna and El Obeid. Service aircraft, shipped to West Africa, were rebuilt by the RAF engineers at Takoradi and ferried to the Middle East and India by RAF pilots. They would then return via BOAC's trans-African air route.

BOAC (Atlantic) Ltd. operated its last round trip of the trans-Atlantic mail service, when long-range Empire Boat G-AFCX 'Clyde' left Poole via Botwood-Montreal-New York on 4th October 1940.

On 19th October 1940, a new service from the UK to West Africa was opened, initially with Short S.30 'C' class flying-boats, substituted with Catalinas and Short S.26 'G' class flying-boats, operating from Poole-Lisbon-Bathurst-Freetown-Lagos. Later flights continued via Leopoldville-

In September 1942 BOAC leased this Lockheed 18-07 Lodestar (c/n 18-2143) from the RAF as G-AGIL 'Lake Nyasa', to operate in Africa and the Middle East and also to fly the Cairo-Gambut-Malta route. It was returned to the RAF in February 1948 becoming HK855.

Coquilhatville-Stanleyville to Lake Victoria, and also to Juba on the White Nile, connecting with the Horseshoe Route from South Africa to Cairo.

Meanwhile, in May 1940, MAP had given BOAC the responsibility of repairing and modifying RAF aircraft, and to overhaul the engines and propellers. Work began at the Croydon and Hythe workshops until the staff and equipment were transferred to new facilities at the Treforest Trading Estate, Pontypridd in June 1940. Two propeller repair shops were also set up in Bath and these repair facilities would form the Propeller and Engine Repair Auxiliary (PERA) from 1st September 1942.

BOAC engineers also assembled 'Lend Lease' aircraft which were shipped to Britain in crates, arriving at Liverpool Docks before being transferred to nearby Speke Airport where the work was carried out until American engineers were able to take over the assembly. A similar facility existed at Colerne, Bath, except the aircraft there were assigned to the RAF.

In the summer of 1940, the MAP also bought U.S. Lockheed Hudsons which needed to be delivered to England. The Canadian Government was asked for urgent assistance and

G-AGFK, a BOAC Vickers Type 456 Warwick C Mk. I (Serial BV256) which was one of fourteen aircraft converted to freighters, displays the wartime colours of BOAC to good effect while flying over England during July 1943. As the aircraft encountered engine problems in service, they were later transferred back to the RAF.

Sir Edward Beatty of Canadian Pacific Railways took up the challenge, forming the Canadian Pacific Air Services (CPAS) at St. Hubert Airfield, Montreal. Mr. G. E. Woods-Humphery, ex-Imperial Airways M.D., assisted Beatty with this new service along with several BOAC managers and four senior pilots - Captains D.C.T. Bennett, A.S. Wilkinson, R.H. Page and I.G. Rose.

On 10th November, seven Hudsons departed from Gander, led by Captain Bennett, arriving safely in Aldergrove, Northern Ireland. RAF pilots took over the task early in 1941 then, in March, the operation was taken over by the Atlantic Ferry Organisation (ATFERO) under MAP. The British Government bought approximately $31 billion of American munitions between 1939-1941, but cash reserves were running out fast. In order to secure further support from the Americans the Prime Minister, Winston Churchill, urged President Roosevelt to continue funding the war effort. His plea was successful resulting in the Lend-Lease Bill HR1776 being passed in Congress on 11th March 1941, allowing Britain to obtain financial and munitions support on credit.

From 4th February 1943 to 18th May 1945, BOAC used Mosquitoes to fly a courier service from Leuchars to Stockholm. A special passenger could be carried in the bomb bay when required, whilst the return cargo was mainly ball bearings, steel springs or resistors. Here we see Mosquito Mk.IV G-AGFV (Serial DZ411) awaiting her next mission.

B·O·A·C 1940~1945

G-AGJA 'Mildenhall', in flight on 14th January 1944, was the first of five Avro York 685s on loan from the RAF. Configured as twelve-seat passenger-cum-freighters (PCF), they introduced the Lyneham-Gibralter-Tripoli-Cairo route alongside RAF Transport Command Yorks. G-AGJA eventually went to BSAAC and became 'Star Fortune'.

As it was found to be too slow and inefficient to return the ferry pilots by ship to Canada, Lockheed Liberators were commissioned to fly the aircrew back and, on the 4th May 1941, Captain Bennett operated the first eastbound Return Ferry Service (RFS) from St. Hubert-Blackpool, and later from Dorval-Prestwick.

From 20th July 1941, the Atlantic Ferry Organisation became known as RAF Ferry Command and they took over the route in partnership with BOAC who operated the flights and maintained the aircraft with the help of Trans Canada Airlines at Dorval. When RAF Transport Command was formed on 25th March 1943, the Atlantic Ferry Organisation became known as No. 45 (Atlantic Transport) Group.

Sweden came under increasing pressure to surrender to the Axis powers despite proclaiming neutrality to the conflict. In February 1941 a route was inaugurated from Leuchars-Stockholm with ex-Polish Airlines (LOT) Lockheed 14 SP-BNF 'Lowicz', now G-AGBG 'Bashful Gertie Terror of the Skagerrak' flying at night.

This was an important route taking urgent mail, supplies and special passengers to neutral Sweden, returning with high quality ball bearings, special tool steel, watch springs, and electrical resistors, all in short supply in England. BOAC later operated this service with Lockheed Hudsons, Whitleys, DC-3s and even the Curtiss Wright C.W.20 G-AGDI 'St Louis' fitted with long-range fuel tanks. First flown in 1940, it was the largest twin-engine aircraft in the world and had a respectable cruising speed of 195mph/314kph.

In 1943 BOAC replaced these various aircraft types with Mosquitoes, one Mk.4 and six Mk.6, the latter powered by two 1,635hp Rolls-Royce Merlin 25 engines which enabled them to cruise at high speed of 300mph/507kph. Initially they flew in daylight but after a Mosquito was attacked by a German Focke Wulf FW-190 fighter and crashed in Sweden, the service reverted back to night-time until the end of the war.

The flights between Norway and Denmark were fraught with danger as not only did the aircraft have to

Avro 685 York 1 G-AGJC 'Malmesbury' sits on a wet ramp at Torslanda Airport Göteborg, Sweden in late 1944. This was BOAC's longest serving York at thirteen years and was one of the last two sold in November 1957 to Skyways.

BOAC inherited twelve of the Armstrong Whitworth A.W. 27 Ensign Mk.I from Imperial Airways and also took delivery of two of the new Ensign Mk.II, one of which is seen here as G-AFZU (c/n AW1821) 'Everest'. They performed sterling work in Europe, Africa, the Middle East and India with nine surviving the war, however they were all scrapped between 1945-1947.

contend with anti-aircraft fire, but also Focke Wulf Fw-90 night fighters, which posed a serious threat to the aircraft. Nevertheless, casualties were minimal with only nine aircraft from 2,100 missions being lost.

On 26th May 1941, the Poole-Foynes-Lisbon-Bathurst-Freetown-Lagos service was flown by the Consolidated Model 28 'Juba' which joined the Empire Boats on the UK-West Africa service. Meanwhile the Boeing 314 Flying Boats undertook a more direct route from Foynes-Lisbon-Bathurst-Lagos, but the aircraft had to be flown to Baltimore in the USA for maintenance after every 120 hours of flying as specialist facilities were not available in Britain. The aircraft were later

committed to the circular route Foynes-Lisbon-Bathurst-Lagos-Bathurst-Belem-Bermuda-Baltimore-Bermuda-Lisbon-Foynes.

Services to West Africa were extended in July the same year, with the Empire flying-boats taking the alternative route via the Belgian Congo to Egypt, from Lagos-Libreville - Pointe Noire - Leopoldville - Coquilhatville-Stanleyville-Butiaba-Port Bell-Juba-Malakal-Khartoum- Wadi Halfa, to Cairo.

In Egypt, at Almaza Heliopolis, the MAP gave BOAC the mammoth task to expand and develop a small overhaul unit into a major facility to repair RAF aircraft operating in North Africa. The Aircraft Repair and Overhaul Unit was established

A rare colour view of Armstrong Whitworth A.W.27 Ensign Mk.II G-ADSU (c/n AW1159) 'Euterpe', freshly painted with camouflage, Speedbird and name, and fitted with new 900hp Wright Cyclone engines, circa 1941.

B·O·A·C 1940~1945

Douglas C-47 G-AGGB (c/n 6227), landing on 10th December 1943, was one of six lend-lease Dakota 1s delivered in March 1943 to BOAC at Whitchurch, Bristol. They initially flew UK to Scandinavia, then in May 1943 to the Iberian Peninsular and North Africa. The UK-Lisbon service replaced KLM DC-3s with a new route, UK-Gibraltar-Rabat-Algiers, later extended to Cairo with up to fifteen services per week.

on 1st August 1941, and by the year end had over 1,000 staff. It was renamed the British Airways Repair Unit (BARU) and continued to expand over the years, employing 4,700 staff before the RAF took control again in March 1944.

In June 1941, Air (Chief) Marshall Tedder, acting as Air Officer Commanding-in-Chief Middle East, organised the 'Tedder Plan' which was implemented by Robert Maxwell, local BOAC Regional Director, in September 1941. This plan, which identified the need for air transport services in Africa as well as transporting ferry pilots back to RAF Takoradi after they had delivered their aircraft, involved BOAC and the RAF in a venture that would use RAF Lodestars on services from Almaza, Cairo to the Sudan, Eritrea, Western Desert, Malta, Turkey and Persia, increasing the frequency of the

trans-Africa supply route. BOAC had also built its own maintenance base at Almaza which opened on 12th October 1941 to service the airline's landplanes operating in the Middle East (40 aircraft consisting of DH.86s, DC-3s, Ensigns, Flamingos, Lockheed Electras, Hudsons, Lodestars, and even four Wellingtons borrowed from the South African Air Force (SAAF) for the Cairo-Karachi service). These aircraft would operate to Addis Ababa, Kamaran and Aden, Khartoum-Malakal-Juba-Kisumu-Nairobi.

On 8th February 1942, Japanese Forces invaded Singapore, thus severing the Horseshoe route which terminated eastwards at Calcutta. A new route opened in April 1942, flown by Lodestars to India along the Hadhramaut Coast to Asmara-Kamaran-Aden-Riyan-Salalah-Masirah-Jiwani and Karachi. The

In 1943/1944 BOAC received 30 C-47A Dakota IIIs followed by 23 Dakota IVs in 1944/1945. Dakota IV G-AGKN (c/n 26429/14948) is seen at Croydon in 1945, carrying the later camouflage and Speedbird symbol. The aircraft operated services from the UK-West Africa, Takoradi-Cairo and Cairo-Karachi.

Boeing 314A G-AGBZ (c/n 2081) 'Bristol' taking off under the power of four 1,600hp Wright Cyclones in 1946. With another two Boeing 314As, 'Berwick' and 'Bangor', they flew Foynes-West Africa, and trans-atlantic services to the USA for maintenance, completing a total of four million miles in six and a half years for BOAC without loss.

previously assigned route to India, flown by the Empire Flying Boats, was replaced by Ensigns and Wellingtons in June the same year, flying from Cairo-Lydda-Habbaniya-Basra-Bahrein-Sharjah-Jiwani to Karachi.

On 21st October 1942, BOAC borrowed an RFS Liberator for a non-stop flight from Scotland to Russia. Captain J. T. Percy, with three crew and eight passengers, took off from Prestwick flying north to the Arctic Circle, across Norway, Sweden, Finland and Poland to Ramenskyoe military airfield, also known as Zhokovsky, 30 miles from Moscow, taking 13hrs 9mins. This route operated in the winter months because of the long nights which gave the crew the added security of darkness over enemy territory. During this first winter, nine successful flights were achieved, with most of the flights command-ed by the famous Captain Gordon Bennett.

To bypass Singapore, an RAF crew flew a BOAC Catalina, G-AGFL, on 3rd November 1942 non-stop from Kogalla Lake, Ceylon-Perth, the first of seven experimental flights. Four additional BOAC Catalinas arrived, modified with long-range fuel tanks as was G-AGFL and, on 10th July 1943, the Catalinas inaugurated a direct service between Ceylon-Australia flown by Qantas crews. The Catalinas carried a maximum payload of 2,204lbs/1,000kgs made up of official dispatches and diplomatic mail, with any spare capacity used in the form of up to three passengers.

The route was extended to Karachi on 30th October 1943 to meet with the BOAC Hythe flying-boat service which operated from 25th October 1943 to the UK via

Three Short S.26 'G' class flying boats were built in 1939 for trans-atlantic mail services. The 'Golden Horn' (c/n S.873) suffered an engine failure on the UK-West Africa service and is seen at Lisbon in January 1943. After repairs, however, an engine fire on the test flight caused the aircraft to crash in the ocean with only one survivor.

B·O·A·C 1940~1945

Twenty-four Sunderlands were de-militarised and fitted with bench seats. They were introduced during March 1943 on the UK-West Africa route and from April 1943 on the UK-Egypt-India route. Here we see Short Sunderland III G-AGIA (Serial ML728) floating on the sea at Southampton.

Cairo, with an estimated flight time across the Indian Ocean of 28hrs non-stop, an amazing feat for the time.

On 17th June 1944, Qantas supplemented the Catalinas with the faster, comfortable Liberators which could carry a greater payload. Liberators also flew 56 flights from the UK to Cairo (Lyneham-Lisbon-Gibraltar-Tripoli-Cairo) between July 1943 and March 1944, before being replaced with Avro Yorks on 20th May 1944 on the service from Lyneham-Rabat-Tripoli-Cairo as they were able to carry larger loads.

A 'Second Front' opened on 7th November 1942 when the Allies invaded Algiers in French North Africa.

BOAC, protected by the British 8th Army, operated a continuous service to the Western Desert using Lodestars, Lockheed 14s and Wellingtons, supplying the 'Second Front' as the Allies attempted to consolidate North Africa, forcing a general retreat on the German army from Egypt.

From 1st March 1943, the first six of BOAC's 25 Short Sunderland Mk. IIIs entered service, flying from Poole via Foynes-Lisbon-Port Etienne-Bathurst-Freetown-Abidjan to Lagos. On 11th July the same year, the Horseshoe route re-opened with Catalinas flown by Qantas Empire Airways under charter to BOAC, flying Ceylon-Australia non-stop in 28 hours (see Qantas). As the Italian resistance began to falter

Douglas C-47A G-AGIU (c/n 12096) was transferred to the British European Airways Corporation from BOAC after becoming surplus to requirements on 1st August 1946.

Above: Armstrong Whitworth AW.27 Ensign Mk.1 G-ADSR (c/n AW1156). Ensign Mk.1s were built with 850hp Armstrong Siddeley Tiger IX engines but were later converted to Mk.2 standard with 950hp Wright Cyclone GR-1820-G102 engines. The Ensign had a wingspan of 123ft/37.49m and length 114ft/34.72m.
Below: A.W.27 Ensign G-ADSY (c/n AW1163) 'Empyrean' is prepared for flight.

and the fighting in North Africa ceased, a service to Moscow began on 10th June 1943, with Liberators flying from Lyneham via Gibralter-Tripoli-Cairo-Habbaniyeh-Persia-Kuibyshev-Ramenskoye.

The first service was flown by the celebrated aviator Captain O. P. Jones and amongst the passengers was the Russian Ambassador to London, Mr Maisky, who helped as interpreter on the flight over Russia.

The Allies invasion of Europe 'Operation Overlord' began on 6th June 1944 across Normandy, France but it was almost a year before hostilities ceased on 8th May 1945 (VE Day).

However, war continued in the Far East and on 6th August a Boeing B-29 Superfortress 'Enola Gay' dropped an atomic bomb 'Little Boy' on Hiroshima, Japan. Three days later, B-29 'Bockscar' dropped a second named 'Fat Man' on Nagasaki. Both cities were destroyed and Japan surrendered on the 15th August 1945 (VJ Day).

BOAC contributed greatly to the war effort, and 80 aircrew were either decorated or received 'The King's Commendation for Valuable Service in the Air'. Many technical

Liberator II G-AGTI (c/n 39), ex-AL541, was bought by BOAC in September 1945 and operated until April 1946. The aircraft was later sold to Qantas for use on the Australia-Ceylon service.

B·O·A·C 1940~1945

Short S.23 Empire 'C' class flying-boat G-AFBL (c/n S.878) 'Cooee' pictured on the Nile at Rod-el-Farag, Cairo.
The last of 31 Short S.23s to be built, she was delivered to QEA as VH-ABF but returned to BOAC
in April 1940. G-AFBL was one of thirteen BOAC Empire boats to survive WWII.

and administration staff were also honoured but the cost was high, with the loss of 36 aircraft and 83 aircrew including 29 Captains. The ATA was closed on the 30th November 1945. Their 1,515 aircrew had flown 147 diverse types of aircraft from fourteen bases, with the loss of 157 men and 16 women.

Also notable were the efforts of PERA who, from 1st September 1942 to 31st March 1945, had repaired 8,250 engines and 22,430 propellers. The RFS continued the North Atlantic crossings after the war and, by 10th February 1946, had completed 2,000 flights.

During the war, BOAC had flown over 55 million miles carrying nearly 275,000 passengers, 7,575 tons of mail and 12,749 tons of cargo whilst operating a total of 160 aircraft of various types. The experience, skills and knowledge gained during WWII would be instrumental in BOAC operating scheduled passenger services across the North Atlantic, with comfortable, fast pressurised Lockheed Constellations in 1946.

Short S.26 'G' Class G-AFCI (c/n S871) 'Golden Hind' was de-militarised in 1945/46 and fitted with a new extended
tail cone, new Bristol Hercules XIV engines, and the cabin was re-configured with 24 first-class seats. It opened a
weekly service Poole-Augusta-Cairo on the 30th September 1946.

Left:
The Smoking cabin.

A selection of interior views of a Short Empire 'C' class Flying Boat demonstrating the luxury interiors of this pre-war flying boat.

Above:
Looking forward in the Promenade Saloon

Left:
Looking aft in the Promenade Saloon

B·O·A·C SPEEDBIRD 1945~1950

The Avro 691 Lancastrian had a cruising speed of up to 290mph/467kph and a range of 4,150 miles/6,679 kms. Lancastrian 1 G-AGLY (c/n 1179) 'Norfolk' flies at altitude on 11th July 1945 during a return flight from Australia.

Although WWII came to an end on 15th August 1945, there was an increase in war traffic with the repatriation of allied prisoners of war from the Far East and the need to transport supplies to military bases in India and the Middle East. The return to peace time conditions was slow. As of 31st March 1946 BOAC, the world's largest airline, had 207 aircraft of eighteen different types including eleven landplanes and seven types of flying-boats, all utilising seventeen different types of engines. Most of these aircraft were uneconomical to operate in peace time conditions except for the DC-3 on short routes and the Boeing 314A on the trans-atlantic route.

On the 23rd December 1942, the British Government had set up the first Brabazon Committee which was chaired by Lord Brabazon of

Tara and included five Air Ministry officials. They were to draft outline specifications for post-war civil transport aircraft and their report of 9th February 1943 recommended five new types and the use of converted military aircraft as a stop-gap.

The second Committee, formed on the 25th May 1943, also included representatives from BOAC and de Havilland and they discussed in greater detail the requirements and specifications of all the aircraft types.

At this point BOAC was surprised to learn that the converted military types would operate for a futher six years and requested permission to purchase American Constellations or DC-4s to compete with PAA and American Overseas Airlines (AOA) on the North Atlantic

Avro 683 Lancaster 1 G-AHVN (Serial PP744) of BOAC's Development Flight at Hurn, which was involved in testing airborne avionics equipment.

Above:

Avro 691 Lancastrian 1 G-AGLS (c/n 1173) 'Nelson' undergoing repairs after a split prop shaft at RAF Tengah, Singapore on 21st September 1947. It was operating the Express Service, Flt. No. 7Q, from the UK-Australia [London-Lydda (13hrs 45min), Lydda-Karachi (13hrs), Karachi-Singapore (13hrs 30min), Singapore-Darwin (11hrs) and Darwin-Sydney (9hrs 30mins)].

Right:

An interior shot of a typical BOAC Lancastrian 1, with three sideway sofas for the use of nine passengers facing towards the starboard windows, with one of three overhead sleeping berths shown lying open.

Below:

Lancastrian 4 G-AKPZ (Serial VL972) 'Nile' sits at Heathrow in the late 1940s.

BOAC SPEEDBIRD 1945~1950

BOAC had nine Lockheed 18-07 Lodestars shipped to Cape Town South Africa which were re-assembled and used on the trans-Africa route, Cairo to Takoradi. G-AGBT (c/n18-2076), named 'Lincoln', had its original 875hp Pratt & Whitney Hornets replaced with 1,200hp Wright Cyclone engines to become a model 18-56. It was sold in 1948 to East African Airways as VP-KFA.

routes. However this request was turned down and BOAC was only allowed to order British aircraft types.

The Brabazon Committee eventually decided on nine new civil transport types which included the Interim Type Avro IIIB and the Avro XXI (Tudor II) for the Empire routes. This was a development of the twelve seat Avro XX (Tudor I) pressurized North Atlantic airliner available from late 1945.

BOAC reluctantly accepted the Tudor II and fourteen of the Tudor I type were ordered by the

Ministry of Supply on 1st November 1944. This was later increased to twenty Tudor I and 30 Tudor II, but the Tudor I had aerodynamic, cabin pressurization and excess weight problems which required 340 extra modifications to the design, thus preventing entry into service until at least 1947.

BOAC also received 21 Lancastrian I long-range aircraft in 1945, with five allocated to Qantas for a joint England-Australia weekly express service. The first scheduled departure on 31st May 1945 operated from Hurn-Lydda-Karachi-Ceylon-Learmouth (Western

This ex-USAAF C-56C Lodestar (c/n 18-2068) was delivered to the RAF via Lagos and became AX720. It was leased by BOAC in July 1941 as G-AGCU 'Lake Kivu' for operations in Africa and the Middle East for several years but was returned to the RAF in November 1947 and later sold in Spain.

Wearing a natural metal livery, BOAC had twelve Handley Page HP.70 Halton 1s. G-AHDU (c/n 1372/SH18C) 'Falkirk' was configured for ten passengers and fitted with large belly freight panniers. The aircraft were introduced on 9th September 1946 on the UK-Cairo route, and later in July 1947 on thr London-Karachi, London-Colombo and London-Accra services.

Australia)-Sydney, the journey taking a total of 63 hours. Due to its popularity, the service was promptly increased to three times per week.

A new service to South America was also planned and, on the 9th October, BOAC Captain O.P. Jones undertook a survey flight in a Lancastrian to Argentina, Chile and Peru in readiness for the new service.

However, the formation of the British South American Airlines Corporation in 1946 put an end to this venture, as the new airline was given Government permission to fly to South America in preference to BOAC.

On the 18th October 1945, the three Boeing 314 flying-boats were transferred to America where they operated from Baltimore to Bermuda three times per week.

Between 1945/46, BOAC took delivery of the Avro York, a new aircraft based on the design of the Lancaster. Avro designed three versions; an all-cargo freighter, a passenger-cum-freighter (PCF) with cargo in the forward compartment and twelve passenger seats in the rear; and an all-passenger version with 24 seats.

BOAC bought 28 of these Yorks, converting eleven into an eighteen-seat configuration, and

Avro 685 York 1 G-AGNL (c/n 1213) 'Mersey' is seen at Heathrow in 1950. BOAC had a fleet of up to 30 Yorks plus nine inherited from the British South American Airways Corporation (BSAAC) in 1949. 'Mersey' was sold to the Lancashire Aircraft Corporation in May 1952.

1945~1950

Short S.45 Solent G-AHIY (c/n S.1311) 'Southsea' in flight over England on 9th April 1948.
The aircraft was built originally as a Mk.2 and later converted to a Mk.3 Solent.

thirteen to twelve-berth sleeper configuration, with the remainder used as freighters. These were used on the new Springbok service to South Africa in partnership with South African Airways (SAA) starting on the 10th November 1945 flying from Hurn, England-Tripoli-Cairo-Khartoum-Nairobi-Johannesburg (Palmietfontein). Nine BOAC Yorks were loaned to SAA until 8th July 1946 when they were replaced with Douglas DC-4 Skymasters.

On 1st January 1946, BOAC formed the British European Airways division to take over European routes from No. 110 Wing of 46 Group RAF Transport Command. The centre of operations transferred from Croydon to Northolt on the 4th February from where BOAC (BEA Division) operated RAF Dakotas to Amsterdam, Brussels, Copenhagen, Helsinki, Lisbon, Madrid, Paris, Stockholm and Rome to Athens. The Dakota aircraft all received civil markings and the crew would wear the standard BOAC uniform with effect from 4th March.

BOAC ordered nine Vickers Viking 1As for their European Division, which later became British European Airways in 1946. One Viking, G-AGRR (c/n 9/109), was used by BOAC's Operational Development Unit at Hurn for testing the Smith's S.E.P.1 autopilot, and radio and radar systems including E.K. Cole Ltd's new weather radar. The aircraft was retired in June 1950.

Lockheed 049E Constellation G-AHEM (c/n 1978) 'Balmoral' is seen in original colours at the Bermuda Air Terminal in 1948. This was one of five bought to inaugurate the post war London-New York service on 1st July 1946.

Twelve Halifax C.8 aircraft, renamed Haltons, were also modified for BOAC with new nose and tail fairings and a large belly freight pannier, whilst the rear fuselage was fitted with large windows and ten individual seats.

The Haltons entered service on the 9th September 1946, flying the UK-Egypt route, but these were withdrawn after only six weeks because of hydraulic problems and the need to install de-icing equipment. They returned to service in July 1947 and operated the UK-Cairo-Karachi service and the UK-West Africa route.

BOAC also converted 23 of their Sunderland III flying boats into the Hythe class, with comfortable accommodation for 24 passengers replacing the former austere interior and hard bench seats previously

carried. The service from the UK-Singapore re-opened on the 31st January 1946, followed by the UK-Australia service on the 12th May (a joint BOAC/Qantas venture), and finally the UK-Hong Kong 'Dragon' service recommenced on the 24th August.

The American Lockheed Model, L-049E Constellation, was the first of a new generation of modern long-range airliners operated by BOAC based at the Dorval, Montreal maintenance facility. Five aircraft were delivered between May and July 1946 and they inaugurated a new trans-atlantic service on 1st July 1946 from London (Heathrow)-Shannon-Gander-New York (La Guardia) taking just under 20hrs westbound.

On 1st August 1946, the Civil Aviation Act 1946

De Havilland DH.104 (c/n 04029) Dove1B before delivery at Hatfield in 1947, in polished metal livery with Speedbird logo. The Doves were used for navigation and flight training.

BOAC SPEEDBIRD 1945~1950

Avro 688 Tudor 1 G-AGRC (c/n 1251) was fitted with 1,770hp Rolls Royce Merlin 621 engines. The Tudor was designed as the first British prop-powered pressurised airliner but was rejected by BOAC in April 1947, although the aircraft was later bought by BSAAC for services to South America.

received Royal Assent, establishing the British European Airways Corporation (BEAC) and the British South American Airways Corporation (BSAAC). Following this, BOAC transferred 21 Dakota aircraft and also its order for the Vickers-Armstrong Vikings to BEAC.

Two Avro Tudor 1s were delivered to BOAC's Development Flight at Hurn during September and November 1946, and flight testing was carried out with the second aircraft in Nairobi for tropical trials. Following these tests, however, BOAC moved towards

rejecting the Tudors because of poor flight performance and range deficiencies, instead accepting a loan of twelve Handley Page Haltons together with the use of Bovington airfield near Hemel Hempstead as a maintenance base. Unbeknown to BOAC, this base was badly maintained and lacked the required heating facilities needed in the hangars.

The Horseshoe service from Durban-Calcutta, flown by 'C' class flying-boats, was reduced in stages, firstly to Calcutta then Cairo until it finally ended on

Above: The interior of an Avro Tudor.
Right: Avro Tudor 1 G-AGRF (c/n 1254) was rejected by BOAC but converted to a Tudor 4B for BSAAC's London-Bermuda route. The Tudor 1 had a maximum cruising speed of 260mph/418kph.

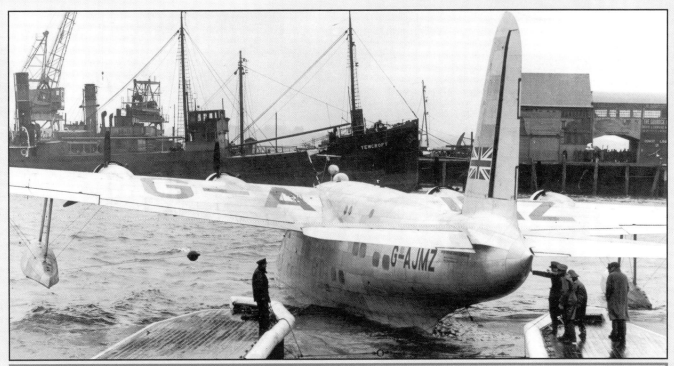

The first arrival at the new Berth 50 at the Southampton Terminal was Short S25/V Sandringham 5 'Plymouth' class G-AJMZ (c/n SH56C) on 31st March 1948, carrying twenty-one passengers from Iwakuni Japan.

the 2nd March 1947. The thirteen 'C' class survivors were flown back to the UK and scrapped.

Meanwhile, HRH Princess Elizabeth had christened Avro Tudor 1 G-AGRF 'Elizabeth of England' at Heathrow on 21st January 1947, but BOAC rejected the Tudor on 11th April because of its lack of range, making it incapable of operating the North Atlantic routes of the airline.

BOAC's Sunderland, G-AGKX, was modified in size to provide for greater passenger numbers and the aircraft, with a streamlined nose and tailcone, was renamed the Sandringham Mk.1. BOAC would also purchase nine Sandringham Mk. 5 'Plymouth' Class aircraft which were configured for 22 day or 16 night passengers. The airline also received three Sandringham Mk. 7 'Bermuda' Class aircraft capable of carrying 30 passengers. Both types were fitted with Pratt and Whitney Twin-Wasp engines.

On the 2nd May 1947, BOAC introduced the Plymouths on the services from Poole-Augusta-Cairo, Poole-Bahrain and Bahrain-Karachi.

The first departure from Berth 50 was Sunderland III Hythe Class G-AGEW (c/n JM665) 'Hanwell', leaving on 1st April 1948 for Sydney, taking five and a half days.

B·O·A·C SPEEDBIRD 1945~1950

BOAC operated twenty-five Handley Page HP.81 Hermes 4s. Here we see G-ALDG (c/n HP81/8) 'Horsa' at the manufacturer's airfield at Radlett in early 1949, wearing the livery that was never carried in service with the airline.

A commercial service from the UK to Canada began on 15th April 1947 using L-749 Constellations from London-Prestwick-Gander-Montreal, followed on the 6th May from London-Shannon-Gander-Montreal. On 1st December 1947, the aircraft were pooled with Qantas for a joint BOAC/Qantas service on the London to Sydney route, whilst the freight service from London to Sydney continued to be operated by the BOAC Lancastrians. These operations were extended when the UK-South Africa freight service began on 11th April 1948.

After a period of two successful years in service on the Baltimore to Bermuda route, the flying boats (Bristol, Berwick and Bangor) were retired on the 17th January 1948, and replaced by Lockheed Constellations, which on the following day opened a new service from Bermuda to New York. During service with BOAC from 15th February 1941, these flying boats had successfully flown five million passenger miles without injury to passengers and crew.

Short Solent flying-boats were introduced on the 4th May from Southampton-Augusta-Alexandria-Khartoum-Port Bell-Victoria Falls-Johannesburg (Vaaldam), replacing the Avro Yorks.

Following the cancellation of the Tudors, BOAC subsequently ordered 22 Canadair C-4 Argonauts

A line-up of Hermes Mk.4s at the manufacturer's airfield at Radlett, Hertfordshire prior to delivery. They were powered by four 2,020hp Bristol Hercules 763 engines giving a cruising speed of 266mph/428kph and carried 40 passengers in first-class comfort.

The second of 22 BOAC Canadair C-4 Argonauts G-ALHD (c/n 146) 'Ajax' prepares to leave Heathrow airport. This is the aircraft which, on 14th June 1949, flew the 26,100 mile proving flight to the Far East.

and Handley Page Hermes for the Empire routes. Also, because of the shortage of modern aircraft for long-haul flights, BOAC bought five Lockheed L-749 Constellations from the Irish airline Aerlinte Eireann for the UK-Australia service, replacing the Hythes on the 1st December 1948.

On the 31st December 1948, Filton in Bristol replaced Dorval as the new BOAC Western Division Constellation base with DC-3s from Whitchurch also transferred to that location. Following the Airways Corporation Act of 1949, BSAAC and BOAC merged and this came into effect on the 30th July 1949.

When Canadair C-4s were delivered to No. 1 Line formed at London Airport, it was split into two flights; an Eastern flight would operate to the Middle and Far East, and a South American flight would commence with ex-BSAAC staff. BOAC operated its first all-landplane service to the Far East on the 23rd August 1949 with a new Canadair C-4 Argonaut, G-ALHJ (c/n 156) named 'Arcturus', flying London-Rome-Cairo-Basra-Karachi-Delhi-Calcutta-Rangoon-Bangkok-Hong Kong, later extended to Japan. A local service also began on 27th August from Singapore to Hong Kong, replacing the Plymouth flying-boats.

In November, the Argonauts replaced the chartered Skyways Ltd. Douglas DC-4s on the London-Rome-Nicosia-Damascus-Abadan route, the weekly service from London-Rome-Damascus-Kuwait-Bahrain, and on the 16th, the London-Rome-Beirut-Damascus-Baghdad route. Yorks

One of four Boeing 377-10-28 Stratocruisers which were bought whilst on the production line from S.I.L.A. (Svensk Interkontinental Lufttrafik A.B.). G-ALSB (c/n15944) 'Champion' sits outside the Brabazon Hangar at Filton in December 1949, carrying the early natural metal livery. They were powered by four Pratt and Whitney 3,500hp R-4360 Double-Wasps which gave a cruising speed of 340mph/547kph.

Lockheed 749A Constellation G-ANVA (c/n 2564) 'Blakeney' at Heathrow.

were also replaced by Argonauts during November on the London-Rome-Lydda route and the London-Rome-Cairo-Bahrain-Karachi-Delhi-Calcutta service and finally, on 16th November, Lancastrians were replaced on the London-Rome-Cairo-Bahrain-Bombay-Colombo-Singapore route. The following year, on 16th March 1950, Argonauts replaced Yorks to South America from London-Lisbon-Madrid-Dakar-Natal-Recife-Rio de Janeiro-Montevideo-Buenos Aires and later to Santiago, Chile.

The first of ten new Boeing Stratocruisers, G-ALSA 'Cathay', arrived at Heathrow on 15th October 1949 and was introduced into service on the London-Prestwick-New York route on the 6th December 1949, followed on the 23rd April 1950 with the London-Montreal service.

The spacious and luxurious 60-seat Stratocruiser soon became a favourite with the passengers who enjoyed the space and comfort, especially the twelve-seat cocktail lounge accessed via a spiral staircase to the lower deck.

The BOAC Annual Report 1949/50 reported that the Corporation operated 79 revenue earning aircraft - Argonauts, Constellations, Lancastrians,

Canadair C-4 Argonaut G-ALHC (c/n 145) 'Ariadne' at Frankfurt-am-Main, Germany in 1952.

Avro 685 York G-AGNN (c/n 1216) was sold to BSAA in 1947, but the aircraft returned when BOAC and BSAA merged in 1949.

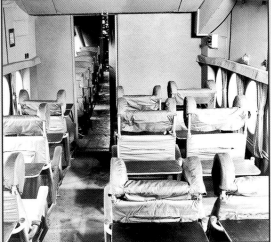

Left and Right: *Two views of the interior of a typical BOAC Avro York, taken in the early 1950s. Although the aircraft was unpressurised, the York proved popular with passengers.*

Solents, Stratocruisers and Yorks. A total of 39 aircraft had been sold in the previous 12 months and another 40 were for sale (many ex-BSAAC). BOAC was in the process of disposing of uneconomic obsolete aircraft and flying-boats and modernising with the latest North American types, along with the purchase of 25 British Handley Page Hermes.

On the 21st January 1947, BOAC had ordered eight Comet 1 jet aircraft. After the merger with BSAAC, this was increased to 14 and the Corporation looked forward eagerly to the delivery of the aircraft in 1951. When delivered, the airline was rightly convinced that the Comet would place BOAC far ahead of the competition which was still using slow and inefficient piston driven aircraft.

Avro 685 York G-AGSO (c/n1239) 'Marston' was one of two Yorks sold to Skyways on 22nd November 1957.

Canadair C-4 Argonaut G-ALHX (c/n 169) 'Astraea' was delivered to BOAC in October 1949 and operated for over ten years until sold to associate company Aden Airways in April 1960 as VR-AAS.

On the 22nd February 1950, BOAC took delivery of the first of twenty Handley Page Hermes 4s which were configured for 40 passengers. The Hermes was then introduced into service on 6th August to replace the Yorks on the UK-West Africa route (London-Tripoli-Kano-Lagos-Accra), and then to East Africa on the 24th September (London-Rome-Cairo - Khartoum - Entebbe - Nairobi) when they replaced the Solents. Six weeks later, on the 7th November, Hermes operated from the UK-South Africa (London-Tripoli-Kano-Brazzaville-Livingstone-Johannesburg) replacing the last Solent service, thus bringing to an end the flying-boat era which had operated for Imperial Airways and BOAC for 26 years.

On the 2nd March 1950, Constellations re-opened the mid-Atlantic route to the Caribbean, flying from London to Lisbon-Azores-Bermuda-Nassau-Havana-Kingston. At Kingston passengers would then transfer to BOAC's last passenger Yorks which operated along the South American West Coast Route to Panama, Lima and Santiago until they were replaced by Connies in October. On the 16th March, the Yorks were also replaced by Argonauts on the

Canadair C-4 Argonaut G-ALHG (c/n 153) 'Aurora' flew the final Argonaut service from Abadan on 8th April 1960.

Two Seaboard and Western Airlines' Lockheed 1049D Super Connies were leased from April 1955 to April 1956, carrying the full BOAC airline livery for services New York-Bermuda and New York-London for a total of three months. Here we see 1049D (c/n 4165) N6503C running up its engines.

South American East Coast Route to Brazil, Argentina and Chile, flying three times a week from London via Lisbon-Dakar-Natal-Recife-Rio de Janeiro-Sao Paulo to Montevideo, Buenos Aires and Santiago.

In August 1950, the reliable Lancastrian freighters operating from the UK to Australia were withdrawn and replaced with Yorks from London-Singapore and then by Qantas Connies from Singapore-Sydney.

BOAC had previously shown interest in the massive ten-engine Proteus turboprop Saunders-Roe SR.45 Princess flying-boat which promised high speed, luxury seating for 100 passengers and with trans-atlantic capability. BOAC's Chairman, Sir Miles Thomas, had visited the Hythe flying-boat base in July 1949 to look at plans drawn up by No. 4 Line

technicians to modify their existing base to accept three Princess boats for servicing and major maintenance with an outlay of less than £100,000. This was quite a feat as the Princess had a wing-span of 219ft 6ins /66.9 metres, length 148ft/45.1 metres and loaded weight of 345,000lbs (154 tons)/156,492 kgs - a bit of a monster even by today's standards.

Early in 1951, BOAC re-evaluated its needs and decided they had no need for the Princesses and the Unit at Hythe was disbanded, however the Government then decided the three aircraft would be used as transport aircraft for the RAF. The prototype G-ALUN would make its first flight on 22nd August 1952, flown by test pilot Geoffrey Tyson off the Solent, although the planned two-three hour flight had to be curtailed because of erroneous

BOAC's first Lockheed 049E Constellation G-AHEJ (c/n 1975) 'Bristol II' taken at Prestwick in 1955 with the short lived large BOAC titles.

1950~1955

Above: *G-AOFI (c/n 04477) de Havilland Dove.*
Left: *G-AIVY Airspeed Oxford 1 (c/n 828) ex-BSAAC joined BOAC'S Central Training Unit's Instrument Flight which was formed at Meadowbank early in 1951. Oxfords and Consuls were eventually replaced with Doves.*
Below: *G-AKCF (c/n 04030) Dove seen in later colours.*

Boeing Stratocruiser Model 377-10-32 G-AKGH (c/n15974) 'Caledonia' was the first of six ordered for BOAC.

instrument readings. G-ALUN would make 46 test flights in total and also appeared at the Farnborough Airshow in 1953, whilst G-ALUO and G-ALUP were built but were destined never to fly. Several offers were made to buy the aircraft and in 1964 they were purchased by Aero Spacelines of the USA who planned to use them as heavy-duty freight aircraft. Unfortunately, when the cocooning was removed they were found to be badly corroded and by 1967 they had all been scrapped after many years of uncertainty in storage.

BOAC had also shown an interest in the eight-engine Proteus turboprop Bristol 167 Brabazon Mk.II which promised luxury non-stop trans-atlantic operation. However the prototype Bristol Centaurus piston-engine Brabazon Mk.1, which was completed and flown in 1949, was felt to be too large and expensive and the aircraft was broken up in 1953 along with the uncompleted Brabazon Mk.II.

BOAC then introduced 'Monarch' deluxe services from London to New York on the 1st March 1951 using Stratocruisers. The Stratocruiser was considered to be one of the most luxurious aircraft ever built with a double-decker seating arrangement, the upper deck having 40-100 seats or 28 sleeper berths, while the lower deck had a lounge and bar.

In March 1952, the BOAC Comet Unit began development trials with three Comet 1s, followed by route proving and training flights to Singapore and South Africa over the next twelve months. On the 2nd May 1952, BOAC introduced the pioneering de Havilland DH.106

Interior views of the luxurious Stratocruiser showing the main deck (left) and lower deck lounge (right).

1950~1955

Handley Page Hermes 4 G-ALDM (c/n H.P.81/14) 'Hero'.

Comet 1 into service on the UK-South Africa route and the inaugural flight, by G-ALYP, carried 36 passengers from London via Rome-Beirut-Khartoum-Entebbe-Livingstone to Johannesburg (Palmietfontein) in 23hrs 34mins. The Comet 1 was then introduced to Asia on 11th August with a service from London-Rome-Beirut-Bahrain-Karachi-Bombay-Colombo, and on 14th October from London-Rome-Cairo-Bahrain-Karachi-Calcutta-Rangoon-Bangkok-Singapore. The following year, on 3rd April 1953, Comets also operated from London-Rome-Beirut-Bahrain-Karachi-Delhi-Calcutta-Rangoon-Bangkok-Manila-Okinawa-Tokyo.

In May 1953 BOAC ordered twelve of the larger 44-seat Comet 2 fitted with Rolls Royce Avon engines

for trans-atlantic operations to South America. A Comet 1 (G-ALYT) was modified with Avons to a Comet 2X and was used by BOAC for proving flights. This aircraft flew to South America on the 13th September, London-Lisbon-Dakar-Recife-Rio de Janeiro-Natal-Dakar-Casablanca-Madrid-London.

The Comet appealed to passengers because of its luxurious quiet interior, combined with smoothness and high speed which reduced travelling time, thereby generating high load factors. However, whilst returning from Singapore on 2nd May 1953, G-ALYV crashed in a severe storm near Calcutta killing all 37 passengers and 6 crew members. The following year, on 10th January 1954, BOAC's first Comet 1 (G-ALYP)

Handley Page Hermes 4 G-ALDI (c/n H.P. 81/10) 'Hannibal' at Nairobi, Kenya.

Hermes G-ALDI (c/n H.P.81/10) 'Hannibal'.

Above Left & Right: *Interior shots of the Hermes.*

Hermes G-ALDP (c/n H.P.81/17) 'Homer' with Hermes G-ALDY (c/n H.P.81/25) 'Honor', and also an Oxford G-AIAU (NM457).

1950~1955

De Havilland DH.106 Comet 1 G-ALZK (c/n 06002) in flight before delivery, 1950.

was 20 minutes into its Rome-London sector when it crashed into the Mediterranean Sea ten miles south of the island of Elba killing all 29 passengers and 6 crew members. The Comet 1s were grounded for investigation, and 60 modifications were authorised and incorporated in each aircraft before they returned to service on 23rd March. Less than two weeks later, however, Comet 1 G-ALYY chartered to SAA crashed into the sea off Naples, Italy on the 8th April 1954 killing all 14 passengers and 7 crew members. At this point Comet 1s were grounded and their Certificate of Airworthiness was withdrawn. This did not deter BOAC, however, who went on to order five of the

long-range Comet 3, stretched to accommodate 58 first-class passengers, for the North Atlantic routes.

BOAC returned four retired Hermes 4s back into service on the East African route on 18th July and increased utilisation of the Argonauts and Constellations. They also bought four more Constellations from Qantas plus one from Trans World Airlines in order to fill the gap in capacity created by the loss of the Comets. The Hermes fleet was then put up for sale in October 1953 as it had been replaced by Argonauts which had been withdrawn from Far East services.

BOAC's first Comet 1 G-ALYS (c/n 06005) at Heathrow on 4th February 1952.

De Havilland DH.106 Comet 1 Prototype G-ALVG (c/n 06001) in BOAC colours at Farnborough in September 1950.

Left & Right:
Two Interior views
of the BOAC Comet 1
fitted with fixed
dining table
and general
main cabin view
looking aft

Comet 1 G-ALYX (c/n 6010) being loaded at Heathrow airport for another service during the early 1950s.

B·O·A·C ⟩ 1955~1960

Above: Douglas DC-7C G-AOID (c/n 45114) on its first flight in 1956 from Santa Monica. Note the undercarriage retracting and the extra long wingspan of 127ft 6in/38.86 metres, 10ft/3.05 metres longer than the DC-7B.

Above: Lord Rennell of Rodd accepting the first of ten BOAC Douglas DC-7Cs, G-AOIA (c/n 45111), at Santa Monica, California on 19th October 1956. DC-7Cs were given the name 'Seven Seas' because of their true non-stop trans-atlantic capability.

BOAC's new centralised HQ at Heathrow, designed by Sir Owen Williams and Partners, opened in stages from 15th July 1955. The dimensions of the structure were 867ft long, 432ft wide and up to 99ft high, and at each of the four corners was a hangar pen with 300ft wide doors, an internal length of 336ft and a depth of 140ft which could accommodate three Stratocruisers, three Britannias or two larger aircraft diagonally with 170ft wing span.

Also within the structure, in a cruciform format segregating the pens on the ground floor, were the stores, aircraft overhaul workshops for power plant, wheels and tyres, propellers, sheet metal electrics, hydraulics, furnishings, machine shops, carpenters' shops and special process shops undertaking battery charging, painting, plating, cabin heating testing, and cleaning bays. The second floor accommodated the Chairman and senior executives, the third floor

Douglas DC-7C G-AOIE (c/n 45115) seen in the early BOAC colours on a test flight in 1957.

accommodated operations staff, and the fourth floor housed the specialised workshops with their controlled environments for testing electrical modules, instruments, radio and radar black boxes. The cafeteria, kitchens, lounge and restaurant were also housed on the fourth floor, whilst the fifth floor contained offices and the sixth floor plant rooms for heating, power and ventilation. By the end of 1955, 4,000 staff worked at the site.

As additional aircraft were needed for the trans-atlantic services, six Boeing Stratocruisers were bought from United Airlines and one (second hand) from Pan American Airways in 1955. However, they required major modifications to bring them up to BOAC's specifications so a number of Lockheed Super Constellations were leased from Seaboard and Western Airlines for the trans-atlantic and daily New York-Bermuda services.

On 30th December 1955, two turboprop medium-range Bristol Britannia 102s were delivered, with five more following in 1956 and the final eight ordered by 12th August 1957, thus completing the contract for Series 102 Britannias

Douglas DC-7C G-AOIC (c/n 45113) taken at Long Beach Field in 1957 before delivery to the airline.

B·O·A·C ▶ 1955~1960

Bristol 175 Britannia Series 102 G-ANBG (c/n 12908), later G-APLL, taken at Filton, Bristol in April 1956.

from the Bristol Aircraft Company. There had been a protracted engine development programme due to engine flame-outs whilst flying in cumulo-nimbus clouds associated with tropical fronts which gave rise to severe ice build-up inside the air intakes on the 180 degree bend. This ice broke off and ingested through the compressors into the combustion chambers, stifling the flame and thus stopping the engine. This was solved by heating

the 'B' skins on the 180 degree bend with jets of air, stopping ice formation and fitting glow plugs to four of the eight combustion chambers which automatically relit the flames.

With the long-range Britannia 300 Series also delayed, BOAC ordered ten Douglas DC-7Cs as a stopgap and the first of these non-stop transatlantic aircraft arrived in October 1956. They

Passengers disembarking from the rear of the Britannia, taken in the early days of service with BOAC. Notice the large turbine engine exhaust pipes and the close proximity of the steps to the nacelles.

Britannia Series 102 G-ANBI (c/n 12910) on a test flight over the Bristol Channel in 1957.

began to operate a London-New York Monarch service on the 6th January 1957, extending to San Francisco on 10th/11th March and, by the summer of 1957, they were operating twenty trans-atlantic services each week.

On 8th November 1956, BOAC signed a contract for the delivery of fifteen Boeing 707s powered by Rolls Royce Conway bypass jet engines and these were destined to enter service in 1960.

Britannia 102 G-ANBI finally flew the first service from the UK to South Africa (London-Rome-Khartoum-Nairobi-Salisbury-Johannesburg) on 1st

February 1957. This was followed on the 2nd March from the UK to Australia (London-Zurich-Istanbul-Calcutta-Singapore-Jakarta-Darwin to Sydney), and on 16th July from London to Tokyo. The Britannia 102s then replaced the Constellations on the London to Aden route in August, London to Colombo in September, and from London to Melbourne on 3rd May 1958.

The long-range Britannia 312 was then introduced into service by G-AOVC which operated the London to New York route on 19th December 1957, the first scheduled turbo-propeller trans-atlantic service, replacing the DC-7C. The Britannia 312, which was

Comet 2E G-AMXD (c/n 06026) taxis out for take-off at the Farnborough Airshow in 1957.

B·O·A·C ➤ 1955~1960

Bristol 175 Britannia Series 102 G-ANBH (c/n 12909) carrying the final BOAC colours worn by the Britannia. She was powered by Bristol Proteus 705s of 3,870hp driving 16ft/4.88 metre diameter propellers and had a cruising speed of 335mph/539kph.

configured with 28 deluxe sleeper seats and 24 first-class seats, operated a non-stop service from London to New York in a scheduled time of 12hrs and from New York to London in 9hrs 50mins.

The following year, on 17th April 1958, Britannia 312s operated from London-Prestwick-Montreal-Detroit-Chicago and on 6th May from London-New York-San Francisco. On 27th July, they replaced the 102s on the London-Rome-Khartoum-Nairobi-Salisbury-Johannesburg route and BOAC then opened their first service to South America in four years with the Britannia 312 operating a twice-weekly service starting on 28th October 1958 from London-Bermuda-Trinidad-Barbados to Caracas. BOAC's faith in the Britannia was justified, as the air-craft was now operating to all Continents and was very popular with passengers because of the space,

Britannia Series 102 aircraft: G-ANBN (c/n 12915) in the early white fin livery and G-ANBE (c/n 12906) sporting the latest colours at Heathrow Airport in the late 1950s.

Britannia Series 312 aircraft: G-AOVB (c/n 13230) and G-AOVF (c/n 13237) on an icy London Airport ramp in February 1958, in company with a Stratocruiser in the background.

Nicknamed 'The Whispering Giant', BOAC ordered eighteen of the long-range Britannia Series 312. G-AOVB (c/n 13230) was the first delivered, powered by four 4,237hp Bristol Proteus 765 engines giving a maximum cruising speed of up to 355mph/571kph.

comfort, smoothness and quietness. It certainly deserved its nickname of the 'Whispering Giant'.

Over the years BOAC had developed many interests around the world with seventeen associated and subsidiary airlines, and the large aircraft maintenance facility called Mideast Aircraft Service Company (MASCO) in Beirut. The situation was complex so BOAC decided to create a holding company called BOAC Associated Companies Ltd. (BOAC-AC) with its own Board to take full responsibility as of 30th November 1957.

Two Comet 2Es loaned to BOAC from the Ministry of Supply, fitted with Rolls Royce Avon Mk.524 jet engines, operated between the UK and Beirut from September 1957 to May 1958. Trans-atlantic routes were also operated to gain experience of the Avon jet engine performance before the Comet 4 (fitted with Avons) came into service.

On 14th January 1958, BOAC signed a contract for 35 Vickers VC10s, which was later reduced to twelve VC10s and seventeen Super VC10s. Then, later that year, the arrival of nineteen of the new Comet 4s began, with deliveries starting on the

Bristol 175 Britannia Series 312 G-AOVG (c/n 13238) is prepared for flight in March 1958.

B·O·A·C 1955~1960

Douglas DC-7C G-AOIC (c/n 45113) sports the final livery carried whilst in the service of BOAC.

12th September 1958 to the final aircraft delivered on 11th January 1960.

Another first for BOAC was the inauguration of the first scheduled jet service across the North Atlantic on 4th October 1958 with Comet 4 G-APDC from London-Gander-New York and Comet 4 G-APDB from New York-London non-stop. Daily services started on the 13th November followed, on 19th December, with a Comet 4 service from London-Gander-Montreal.

The following year Comet 4s opened a jet service

Boeing Stratocruiser 377-10-34 G-ANUB (c/n 15969) 'Calypso' is surrounded by building workers at Heathrow airport in the late 1950s.

Above: The old and the new - de Havilland DH.106 Comet 4 G-APDM (c/n 6414) is towed past a company Stratocruiser at Heathrow in 1959.

from London to Singapore on 1st June 1959 replacing the Britannia. With a reduction in freight carriage from the Britannia to the smaller Comet, additional cargo capacity was required so an agreement was signed with Skyways Ltd. of London to operate 'The Skyways Freight Service'. The London to Singapore and London to Hong Kong routes were operated initially with their ex-BOAC Handley Page Hermes 4, which were later replaced with ex-BOAC L-749 Constellations until

1962, when they were replaced again with two of BOAC's company owned DC-7F freighters.

On 31st March 1959, Bristol Britannia 312 Series G-AOVT left Heathrow on a round-the world service from London-New York-San Francisco-Honolulu-Tokyo at the same time as Comet 4 G-APDH inaugurated the eastward round-the-world service. Later in the year BOAC also signed a Boeing 707 equipment, spares,

Below: An interesting line up of BOAC aircraft at Heathrow, including a de Havilland DH.106 Comet 4, Boeing 377-10-32 Stratocruiser G-AKGM (c/n15979) on lease to Nigeria Airways, with two more Stratocruisers behind.

B·O·A·C 1955~1960

Above:
Comet 4 G-APDM (c/n 6414) seen in its final BOAC livery outside the huge hangars of Technical Block 'A', originally BOAC H.Q. Heathrow. The Comet was sold to MEA in March 1967 and re-registered OD-AEV. It was later leased to Malaysia-Singapore Airlines in January 1968 as 9V-BBJ.

Right: A view of the first-class section of a BOAC Comet 4.

Below:
Comet 4 G-APDG (c/n 6427) undergoes a maintenance check at Heathrow in April 1964. It was sold to Kuwait Airways as 9K-ACI in December 1966.

Above: *Canadair CL-44D4-1 (c/n 31) N228SW.*

and tools pooling agreement with Air France, Pan American, Qantas and Trans World Airlines which would ease the constant spares supply problems for the aircraft at 32 stations worldwide. By the following year, these contracts had mushroomed to thirteen airlines at 65 stations around the globe.

Right:
CL-44D4-1 (c/n 31) N228SW during the process of opening its enormous rear door.

Below:
To fulfil a need for dedicated freighters, two DC-7Cs were modified to DC-7Fs by Douglas Aircraft at Santa Monica in September 1960. These were BOAC's last piston-engined aircraft, with the last flight by G-AOIJ from Hong Kong-London on 14th October 1964. G-AOII (c/n 45119) sits at Heathrow in June 1962.

B·O·A·C ➤ 1960~1969

Boeing 707-436 G-APFE (c/n 17706) was powered by four 17,500lbs static thrust Rolls-Royce Conway 508s and was fitted with two H.F. probe antennas, one on top of the fin and the other on the starboard wingtip.

During 1960 the Comet 4s and Britannias were operating successfully, Boeing 707s and Vickers VC10s were on order, whilst the Stratocruiser and Argonauts were retired.

A return to South American service resumed on 25th January with Comet 4s operating from Heathrow-Madrid-Dakar-Sao Paulo-Montevideo-Buenos Aires-Santiago, whilst Britannia 312s were operating from Heathrow-Bermuda-Barbados-Trinidad-Caracas-Bogata twice weekly. During the year, BOAC signed several partnership agreements starting on 1st March 1960 with an agreement with Trans-Canada Air Lines for UK-Canada services. One month later, on 1st April, a tripartite agreement was signed with Air India and Qantas for services between the UK and India, the Far East and Australia. This was followed on 1st October when a quadripartite African Partnership was agreed with CAA, EAAC and SAA for services from London via Central and East Africa to Johannesburg. A pool agreement was also signed on 1st October with British United Airways for 'Skycoach' services from the UK to Central and East Africa.

Boeing 707-436 G-APFM (c/n 17714) at Heathrow Airport on 16th November 1960 in its original BOAC colours. It later operated under BOAC-Cunard from 1962 - 1966, before returning to BOAC.

BUA Viscount Series 831 G-APNE (c/n 403) chartered by BOAC for use on the Glasgow-Edinburgh-Prestwick shuttle.

An important day for BOAC was 29th April 1960 when their first Boeing model 707-436, registered G-APFD, was delivered to London (their first two G-APFB and G-APFC were undergoing final preparation in the USA). The 707s were introduced into service on 27th May from London direct to New York, and on 1st June from the UK to Canada. Additional 707 services operated on 20th September to Detroit and Chicago, extended on 20th October to San Francisco then, on 8th December 1960, Boeing 707s operated across the Pacific from San Francisco-Tokyo-Hong Kong.

The Comet 4s were finally retired from scheduled North Atlantic operations with the last New York to London flight taking place on 16th October 1960. They were then transferred to secondary routes and also made available for leasing to Associated Airlines.

BOAC's two dedicated Douglas DC-7F freighters operated a North Atlantic cargo service from Heathrow-Manchester-Prestwick-Montreal-New York from 3rd December 1960 until replaced in October 1963 with a Canadair CL-44D4-1 freighter leased for two years from Seaboard World Airlines of the USA. The DC-7F freighters were operated on other routes until retirement on14th October 1964.

Eagle Airways (Bermuda), which became Cunard Eagle Airways (Bermuda), obtained a route licence from the UK to Bermuda for Skycoach services with Britannias in October 1960. As BOAC did not want to compete in this small market, they

Boeing 707-436 G-APFI (c/n 17710), displaying a new style BOAC logo, is pushed back at Heathrow in May 1962.

BOAC ➤ 1960~1969

Boeing 707-436 G-ARRC (c/n18413) in the new Golden Speedbird livery at Heathrow on 26th April 1964.

reluctantly signed a pool agreement effected on 15th April 1961 for the UK to Bermuda route.

On 20th June 1962, BOAC-Cunard Ltd. (BCL) was formed with BOAC holding 70% stock and the Cunard Steam-Ship Company 30% (they bought around 60% of Eagle Airways on 21st March 1960 which became Cunard Eagle Airways) to operate the majority of scheduled services across the Atlantic from the UK to the western hemisphere. Their eleven 707-436s were later joined by two 707-336C freighters and four Super VC10s, with the

aircraft bearing the BOAC livery with additional BOAC Cunard titles on the nose.

The Britannia 102s began to be phased out from November 1962 and were stored at Cambridge for onward resale. BOAC reserved places for six American SSTs on 23rd January 1963, but this aircraft was never built. The Vickers VC10 went into scheduled service on 29th April 1964 from London to Lagos operated by G-ARVJ, followed a year later on the 1st April 1965 with the inaugural flight of the first of four Super VC10s into

The Golden Speedbird livery was introduced in 1964 when the VC10 entered service with BOAC and BOAC-Cunard. It also appeared on 707s (see opposite) and at least one Super VC10, but was unfortunately short-lived, believed to be due to the cost of up-keep of its maintenance. Here we see a close-up of 707-436 G-ARRC (c/n 18413) before entering service at Heathrow.

VC10 G-ARVC (c/n 806) flies at altitude in December 1964.

service on BOAC-Cunard's most important route from London to New York non-stop. The Super VC10 was specifically advertised as 'Triumphantly swift, silent, serene'.

The twelve standard VC10s and seventeen Super VC10s replaced the Britannias with G-AOVL flying the last BOAC Britannia 312 service on 26th April 1965. Following the Britannia, the Comet 4s were eventually retired in November 1965, with many sold to BOAC associated companies.

Two B707-336C freighters were delivered to BOAC-Cunard on 17th December 1965 replacing the leased Flying Tiger CL-44, and later additional B707 freighters were acquired in November 1967, June 1968, and a futher two in March 1970.

During March 1966, BOAC's capital was restructured under the Air Corporation Act and Speedbird House opened at Heathrow in May for the accommodation of Head Office staff. A commercial agreement was signed in July with Iranair for joint services between Tehran and London.

In September 1966, six Boeing 747-136s were ordered, later increased to twelve in November 1968. The Cunard Steam-Ship Company, which had to raise 30% of the cost of the new 747s, had suffered strikes and a downturn in traffic in 1966. As they needed extra capital to keep the company going, they decided to sell their 30% stake in BOAC-Cunard and at the last BCL Board Meeting in September 1966, BOAC paid the Cunard Steam-Ship Company a total of £11.5 million for their shares.

Boeing 707-465 G-ARWD (c/n 18372) carries the short-lived BOAC-Cunard livery at Mexico City on 5th April 1966.

➤BOAC 1960~1969

Standard VC10 G-ARVJ (c/n 812) prepares to launch the first revenue service for BOAC from Heathrow, London to Lagos, Nigeria on 29th April 1964.

An agreement was made during 1966/67 for administration and commercial staff to be seconded to the Kingdom of Libya Airlines, and expansion continued on 1st April 1967 with a new route across the South Pacific from London-New York-San Francisco-Honolulu-Fiji-Sydney. BOAC's engine overhaul factory at Treforest, South Wales became the BOAC Engine Overhaul Limited (BEOL) Company on 1st April 1967 and now traded inde-

pendently. Another new pool agreement was signed, this time with Saudi Arabian Airlines for the BOAC London to Jeddah weekly service. More new commercial agreements were signed, starting in 1968/69 with Viasa on the London to Caracas route and in 1969/70 with Aeroflot on the London to New York and Moscow to Tokyo routes. Another new route for the BOAC 707s was from London-Anchorage-Osaka via the north pole on 5th May 1969.

A rare shot of Super VC10 G-ASGB (c/n 852) at Johannesburg carrying the short-lived Golden Speedbird livery.

Super VC10 G-ASGD (c/n 854) of BOAC-Cunard.

Two interior views of BOAC VC10 G-ARVC (c/n 806). **Left:-** The First Class cabin. **Right:-** The Economy Cabin.

The first Super VC10, G-ASGA (c/n 851), seen in late 1965 during flight testing at Wisley, the Vickers' test centre south of the Weybridge production plant. G-ASGA was operated by BOAC, later BA, until April 1981 when sold to the RAF. It was modified to a K.Mk.4 tanker and given the Serial ZD230.

BOAC 1969~1974

BOAC-Cunard introduced jet freight services on the North Atlantic route with two Boeing 707-336Cs in January 1966.

During 1969 the shipping company British and Commonwealth, who owned British United Airways, entered into intensive negotiations with BOAC with a view to selling the airline to the state carrier. Later that year, BOAC agreed to purchase BUA unaware that the British Government would, at the last minute, veto the sale.

In readiness for the Jumbo Jet's arrival, a new hangar (named 01) and workshops to accommodate two Boeing 747s were built at Heathrow by 12th March 1970. This was followed by the new BOAC Cargo Centre, opened also at Heathrow by HRH The Duke of Edinburgh on the 22nd May 1970. The first of twelve Boeing 747-236s arrived on 23rd May

1970 followed by a futher five, but unfortunately these were destined to sit on the ground because of protracted negotiations between BOAC and the Pilots' Union BALPA. In fact, the 747 inaugural service from London-New York-Bermuda did not occur until the following year, on 14th April 1971.

On the 9th September 1970, flight BA775 operated by Super VC10 G-ASGN was hijacked in flight by the Palestine Liberation Organisation (PLO) and forced to land, initially in Beirut, then later flown to Dawson's Field in Jordan where all the passengers were eventually disembarked safely. Three days later, the aircraft was blown up and destroyed. Later that month there was better

Left:
An interesting line-up at JFK Airport in April 1965:
Super VC10 G-ASGD (c/n 854), Boeing 707-436 G-ARWE (c/n 18373), and Britannia 312 G-AOVL (c/n 13420).

Boeing 707-365C G-ATZD (c/n 19590) landing at Heathrow in March 1972.

news when BOAC's new passenger terminal at JFK Airport in New York was officially opened by HRH Princess Alexandra on 24th September 1970. The terminal's cost was shared with Air Canada and used also by BWIA and Qantas.

BOAC reserved positions for Concorde and their Project Team started to review Concorde maintenance at Filton. It was a long time coming but on 25th May 1972, BOAC

BOAC chartered two Cambrian Airways' Viscounts which linked Belfast and Edinburgh to Prestwick for connecting with BOAC's trans-atlantic services. Viscount V.701 G-AMON (c/n 27) 'Scottish Princess' is seen above in 1972.

BOAC's aircraft sitting idle during a work-to-rule, but a BOAC Reliant Robin is on the move.

➤ BOAC 1969~1974

Vickers VC10s galore, with a lone Boeing 707, on the BOAC maintenance ramp at Heathrow in January 1972.

ordered five Concordes, with a contract signed with British Aircraft Corporation/Aerospatiale on 28th July 1972.

The outcome of the Edwards Committee Report on British Civil Aviation was a recommendation that a British Airways Board be established to review the affairs of BOAC and BEA and report to the Secretary of State. The outcome, under Section 57 of the Civil Aviation Act 1971, was that BOAC be dissolved on 31st March 1974. The Air Corporation's (Dissolution) Order 1973 was effected on 1st April 1974 and this transferred all of BOAC's and BEA's property rights and liabilities to the British Airways Board. The new airline was to be known as British Airways (resurrecting British Airways of 1935).

And so ended the BOAC Speedbird - gone but not forgotten. BOAC operated to first-class standards over a total of 34 years and achieved some of the highest load factors and regard by passengers flying with any airline worldwide. It is no surprise that even today, BOAC is still remembered with great affection by those who either served the company or flew in the aircraft.

The final type to enter service with BOAC was the Boeing 747. BOAC's first 747-136 (c/n 19761) is seen on a test flight from Seattle, wearing the registration N17998. When issued with its British 'Certificate of Airworthiness', it was registered G-AWNA.

1944~1949

Avro 683 Lancaster Mk.I Freighter G-AGUL (s/n PP690) 'Star Watch' was fitted with a Lancastrian cargo nose for the transportation of passenger luggage in 1946.

On 26th January 1944, British Latin American Air Lines Ltd. (BLAAL) was registered at 14, Leadenhall Street, London EC3, with capital of £10,000 under the chairmanship of John Wells Booth. Founded by five British shipping companies, the shareholding was as follows; Royal Mail Lines Ltd. of London 38%; Blue Star Line Ltd. of London 19%; Pacific Steam Navigation Co. of Liverpool 19%; Lamport and Holt Line Ltd. of Liverpool 9%; the Booth Steamship Co. Ltd. Liverpool 5% and BLAAL Chairman John Wells Booth holding 5%. The remaining shares were held by five BLAAL directors with each receiving 100 shares. On 13th September 1945, a special resolution was passed to change the name to British South American Airlines Ltd. (BSAA) with the Certificate of Change issued on 3rd October 1945.

In October 1945, a joint BOAC/BSAA survey flight was undertaken to South America with Capt. O. P. Jones in command of BOAC Lancastrian G-AGMG. When Heathrow Airport was officially opened on 1st January 1946, the honour of the first departure went to BSAA Lancastrian Mk.3 G-AGWG 'Star Light' commanded by Air Vice-Marshall D.C.T. Bennett on the first of six proving flights to Argentina via Lisbon-Bathurst-Natal-Montevideo-Buenos Aires. The flights proved successful and the route was inaugurated on 15th March by Lancastrian G-AGWK 'Star Glow', taking three days and six hours. Only three months later, on 27th June 1946, it became a weekly service and the route was extended from Buenos Aires to Santiago, Chile through the high passes of the beautiful but dangerous Andes range avoiding Tupungato (22,310ft / 6,800m) and Aconcagua (22,835ft / 25.080m).

On 1st August 1946, British South American

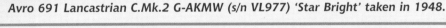

Avro 691 Lancastrian C.Mk.2 G-AKMW (s/n VL977) 'Star Bright' taken in 1948.

1944~1949

Avro 688 Tudor IV G-AHNN (c/n 1347) 'Star Leopard' in flight in February 1948.

Airways Corporation (BSAAC) and British European Airways Corporation (BEA) became public corporations under the 1946 Civil Aviation Act. The Government retained Mr. J.W. Booth as BSAAC's Chairman and the registered office was at 19 Grafton Street, London with a maintenance base at Langley near Slough. It was reported that BSAAC's fleet consisted of four Lancaster freighters, six Lancastrians and four Yorks, with the operational base being Heathrow. On 2nd September 1946, a new fortnightly service was opened by Lancastrian 'Star Guide' G-AGWL from London via Santa Maria (Azores), Bermuda and Jamaica to Caracas, extended to Lima and Santiago on 18th January 1947, whilst Avro Yorks operated a weekly service from London-Lisbon-Dakar-Natal-Rio de Janeiro from 12th October 1946.

In August 1947 BSAAC bought 47% shares in British West Indian Airways (BWIA) and another 28% on 1st October 1947 through British

International Airlines (BIA), a BSAAC subsidiary. The Avro Tudor 4 was introduced on the mid-Atlantic route from London-Lisbon-Azores-Bermuda-Nassau to Havana on 31st October 1947 and this was followed with the Yorks, based at Nassau, inaugurating a Nassau-Miami service three times per week from 1st February 1948 and Nassau-Havana from 21st August 1948. Unfortunately, on 30th January 1948, after only four months in service, Tudor G-AHNP 'Star Tiger' disappeared between the Azores and Bermuda.

Hopes were high in 1947 and BSAAC ordered six Comet 1s (although never built) and showed an interest in the Saro Princess flying boats. The company continued to expand in the Caribbean and bought Bahamas Airways in August. The following year, however, on the 17th January 1949, another Tudor G-AGRE 'Star Ariel' also vanished without trace between Bermuda and Kingston, Jamaica and following a Committee of Inquiry

Avro 685 York G-AHFE (c/n1308) 'Star Vista' wears BSAA's stylish livery.

1944~1949

Above: *One of four Avro 683 Lancaster Mk.I freighters, G-AGUM (s/n PP757) named 'Star Ward',*
was modified with the addition of a long belly pannier for outsize freight.

into these accidents, the Tudor 4s were grounded.

It was decided to merge BSAAC with BOAC and on the 1st July J.W. Booth became joint BOAC Deputy Chairman along with Whitney Straight. The Airways Corporation Act 1949 received Royal Assent on the 30th July 1949 and BSAAC shares were transferred to BOAC on 14th October 1949. BSAA remained dormant until 11th March 1971 when it became British Overseas Air Charter Ltd. for BOAC's non-IATA charter operations. The company was then renamed BOAC Ltd. on the 11th December 1989 and continued to operate charter services until it ceased trading on 31st March 1997.

Above: *Avro 19 Anson Series 2 G-AIKM (c/n 1364) 'Star Visitant'*
operated tranport duties.
Below: *Airspeed AS.65 Consul G-AIUX (c/n 5106) 'Star Master' was used for*
training and joined BOAC's Training Unit at Hurn, then later the Central Training
Unit Instrument Flight, Meadowbank, London Airport in 1951.
The Consul was sold to East African Airways as VP-KMI in 1954.

1955~1959

ALITALIA

In the late 1940s, Alitalia Lancastrian Mk.3 I-AHBY served the airline on long distance services to South America for approximately two years.

Aerolinee Italiane Internazionali (Alitalia) was formed in Rome on 16th September 1946 by the Italian Government (47.5%), British European Airways (40%) and Italian investors (12.5%). Revenue operations started on 7th May 1947 with Fiat G.212s and Savio-Marchetti SM-95s from Rome to Catania-Naples-Turin-Cairo-Lisbon, and in 1948 to Geneva, London, Nice and Paris.

Five Lancastrian Mk.3s bought through BEA were inaugurated into weekly service on 2nd June 1948 from Rome-Dakar-Natal-Rio-Sao Paulo-Montevideo-Buenos Aires, but were replaced in 1950 with four Douglas DC-4s which flew Rome-Lisbon-Azores-Fort de France-Caracas and in 1951 to New York. An initial four Douglas DC-6Bs were introduced to the fleet in 1953/54 as well as four Convair CV-340s.

On 31st March 1955, BOAC bought 20,000 Alitalia shares from BEA and within a year increased its holding to 45,000 shares at 10,000 Lire, valued at £321,630. Alitalia continued expansion in 1956 by adding two Convair CV-440s followed, in 1957/58 with four DC-7Cs for trans-atlantic and South African services. On 1st September 1957, Linee Aeree

Douglas DC-4 I-DALV (c/n 10351) 'Citta di Napoli' was built as a C-54A for the USAF but was converted to a DC-4 and flew with PAA, 20th Century Airlines and Alitalia. The aircraft was sold to Air Charter as G-AOFW and later served with BUA who converted it to an ATL-98 Carvair.

1955~1959

At Santa Monica in 1950, Douglas DC-6 I-LADY (c/n 43216) awaits delivery to Linee Aeree Italiane (LAI) of Italy, the airline which eventually became Alitalia.

Italiane was merged with Alitalia adding six Vickers Viscounts and five Douglas DC-6Bs. Alitalia at this point bought six Douglas DC-7Cs during 1957/58 for South African and trans-atlantic operations.

By 1958/59, BOAC had sold their Alitalia shares to British European Airways.

Alitalia bought four Convair Liner 340s in 1953/54 which were later converted to 440s and then joined by two new 440s in 1957. Convair Liner I-DOGI (c/n 340-63) was delivered in March 1953 and remained in service for eight years until sold to Finnair as OH-LRG in March 1961.

Douglas DC-7C I-DUVE (c/n 45229) on a test flight in the USA in November 1957.

1946~1952

Douglas C-47 EI-ACH (c/n 12893), ex-USAF, approaching Heathrow in August 1956.

On 5th April 1946, an agreement was signed between the UK and Eire Governments for air services between the two countries to be operated by Aer Lingus, which was owned by the Irish Government through Aer Rianta holding 60%, BEA 30% and BOAC 10%. Services under this agreement began on 1st July with DC-3s flying Dublin to Croydon (later Northolt) and DH.86s and DC-3s from Dublin to Liverpool.

On 26th February 1947, Aer Rianta founded subsidiary Aerlinte Eireann to operate trans-atlantic services to the USA and ordered five Constellations. The first of seven Vikings arrived on 4th June and operated from Dublin-Manchester-Amsterdam and Dublin-London then, on 17th September, the first of three Constellations arrived. However the trans-atlantic service was postponed and so they were operated from Dublin to Heathrow from 3rd November, and Dublin to Rome from the 12th November.

In 1948, the airline suffered heavy losses and the Vikings were sold to the UK and Egypt and the Connies sold to BOAC. Operations continued however with DC-3s and a DC-3 freighter service from Dublin to Glasgow, Bimingham and Liverpool with Bristol Freighters joining the fleet in March 1952. BOAC sold their shares to BEA in July 1952.

Bristol 170 Freighter Mk.31 EI-AFP (c/n 12827) wearing the early colours of Aer Lingus in 1952.

1946~1952

Top: *Aer Lingus had seven Vickers-Armstrong V.634/1B Vikings. Seen at Northolt Airport, London is EI-ADI (c/n 211) named 'St. Mel', which was bought new in July 1947 and sold to Airwork in February 1948. The colour scheme was dark green with an orange outline to the cheatline.*

Above: *Lockheed 749A Constellation EI-ACS (c/n 2549) 'Padraig' was delivered new in August 1947. The five Aerlinte Connies were later sold to BOAC in June 1948. EI-ACS became G-ALAL and was re-named 'Banbury' whilst the name 'Padraig' (Saint Patrick) was reused many times by Aer Lingus.*

Right: *Aer Lingus operated two de Havilland DH.86Bs. Seen in close-up is EI-ABK (c/n 2338) 'Eire'. It was sold in the UK as G-ADVJ and turned up with Gulf Aviation in 1950 where it operated for a short time until retired from use in March 1952.*

1950~1959

Douglas C-47A G-AKII (c/n 12299) 'Salamis' displays the airline's early livery in 1948.

On 24th September 1947, Cyprus Airways Ltd. was incorporated in Nicosia and a share capital of £125,000 was issued, with BEA holding 44.5% and the remainder being held by the Cypriot Government and local investors.

On 6th October 1947, BEA operated the first services between London-Marseilles-Rome-Athens, and Athens-Nicosia under charter to Cyprus Airways. The airline then acquired three C-47As via BEA in March 1948 to inaugurate services from 18th April between Nicosia-Alexandria-Cairo, Nicosia-Ankara-Istanbul and Nicosia to Athens, Beirut and Lydda. In 1949 the share capital was increased to £185,000 with BEA holding 46% until 1950, when 23% was transferred to BOAC.

By 1951 the fleet had expanded to six C-47s and two Auster J/5s for crop spraying. New routes were added from Nicosia-Ankara, Nicosia-Port Sudan-Khartoum, Nicosia-Rome, and Nicosia-Baghdad-Kuwait-Bahrain.

On 7th June 1952, BEA introduced the Airspeed Ambassador (Elizabethan Class) on a weekly London-Rome-Athens service continuing to Nicosia as a Cyprus Airways flight. In 1953 two ex-BOAC Airspeed Oxfords were bought for training, and the Ambassadors were replaced by Viscount 701s (Discovery Class) on the Athens-Nicosia route on 18th April, followed by Nicosia-Beirut a year later in 1954 and Nicosia-Tel Aviv in 1956.

The Viscounts were popular and a further two were ordered for delivery in 1957, however the order was cancelled because of the cost and political unrest on the island. The Austers and obsolete DC-3s were sold and Cyprus Airways signed a five year agreement with BEA to take over operation of the network from 26th January 1958 using Viscount 806s.

BOAC sold their 23% shareholding to BEA in March 1959 and BEA, in turn, sold them to the Cyprus Government at nominal cost.

BEA Elizabethans operated Athens-Nicosia routes for Cyprus Airways from 7th June 1952.

AIR JAMAICA 1963~1969

Boeing 707-436 G-APFF (c/n 17707) wearing Air Jamaica stickers at JFK on 16th May 1967.

Air Jamaica was formed in August 1963 in partnership with BOAC (33%), BWIA (16%) and the Government of Jamaica (51%). Services began on the 1st May 1966 when BOAC Boeing 707s and BWIA Boeing 727s operated from Jamaica to Miami and New York.

Air Jamaica ceased operating on the 31st March 1969 and was taken over by Air Jamaica (1968) Ltd. in which BOAC had no interest.

Boeing 727-78 9Y-TCO (c/n 18794) at Palisadoes Airport, Kingston on 23rd April 1967.

1949~1970

DH.114 Heron 2 VP-BAP (c/n 14088) in flight in December 1955.

Bahamas Airways Ltd. (BAL) was founded in December 1936 by The Hon. H.G. Christie and Sir Harry Oaks based at Nassau, New Providence, Bahamas. Charter flights operated to the outer islands using an eight seat twin-engined Douglas Dolphin amphibian, and in January 1941 a weekly service from Nassau-Eleuthera was operated by a baby Grumman.

Pan American Airways (PAA) purchased 45% of BAL shares on 10th December 1943 and BAL acquired three ex-PAA Consolidated Commodore flying boats (22 seats) which operated services to Grand Bahama, Eleuthera and Long Island.

BSAAC then bought BAL's stock in August 1948, followed in October when they purchased PAA's 45% share, taking over BAL with a mixed fleet of one Consolidated Commodore, one Catalina flying-boat, two Grumman Goose amphibians and a Seebee amphibian. They still operated schedules to the outer islands but also operated charters to Cuba, Florida, Jamaica and Haiti and later, in 1949, to Havana.

The merger of BSAAC with BOAC was effected on 30th July 1949 (Airways Corporation Act 1949). BSAAC already had a 75% share holding in BWIA from 1st October 1947, and BOAC now had a large presence in the West Indies. BAL then acquired two ex-British Caribbean Airways' DC-3s but losses built up steadily over the next few years and in the 1951/52 financial year, the deficit was £101,688. At the end of 1951, BAL was downsized and all

Grumman G.21A Goose VP-BAA (c/n 1007) 'Andros' awaits its next task in 1955.

1949~1970

Douglas C-47B VP-BBM (c/n 25623/14178) taken at Nassau on the 9th March 1963.

international routes were transferred to BOAC/BWIA with flights operated by BOAC Connies and Stratocruisers and BWIA Vikings. Only the inter-island routes, operated with amphibians, were retained by BAL and in May 1952 the two C-47 Dakotas were sold to BWIA, reducing the deficit to £14,452. During 1956/57 BAL was modernised and the local network extended, with two Heron Mk.2 convertible 14/17-seat landplanes (VP-BAO and VP-BAP) delivered in late 1955 and another, VP-BAN, delivered in December 1956.

By March 1959 the deficit had soared and the two Herons were sold to BWIA. BOAC sold 80% of their shares to Skyways (Bahamas) Ltd. who supplied two DC-3s and leased two ex-BOAC Handley Page

HP.81 Hermes 4s, with one replaced later due to damage (see Gallery photo). The Hermes operated international routes from Nassau to Miami, West Palm Beach and Fort Lauderdale but although they attracted satisfactory loads, losses rose again to £400,000. BOAC then re-purchased the 80% shares sold to Skyways and the Hermes were replaced with two ex-BWIA Viscounts. Two Goose amphibians were also replaced by two Aero Commanders.

When BOAC-Cunard was formed in June 1962, the international services of Bahamas Airways and Cunard Eagle Airways (Bahamas) were integrated. The latter airline used two Viscounts of Cunard Eagle Airways (Bermuda) which went to the new Bahamas Airways and four turboprop H.S.748s

Viscount V.707 VR-BBH (c/n 32) awaits passengers at Nassau on 1st March 1963.

1949~1970

HS.748 Series 2 VP-BCM (c/n1612) in flight in April 1967.

were delivered in 1967. However, costs increased and profits reduced and so BOAC sold 85% of Bahamas Airways to the Swire Group of Hong Kong in 1968. Two turbo-jet BAC 1-11s were introduced but losses continued over the next two years and the airline went into liquidation on 9th October 1970. BOAC's 15% shareholding was considered then as worthless.

Bahamas Airways bought two Aero Commander 500As, VP-BCA and VP-BCB, to replace two Grumman Goose amphibians in October 1962. One of the aircraft, VP-BCA (c/n 500 A-908-17), is caught idle at Nassau on the 9th March 1963. In June 1967 the aircraft was sold in the USA, taking on the registration N543AN.

1949~1967

Shorts S.A.6. Sealand VP-TBA (c/n SH1565) 'St Vincent' at Farnborough in 1949.

British West Indian Airways (BWIA) was established on the 27th November 1939 in Port-a-Spain by Lowell Yerex, a New Zealand pilot who had also formed Transportes Aereos Centro-Americanos (TACA) in Honduras during 1931. Scheduled services began on the 26th November 1940 with an ex-TACA Lockheed model 18-07 Lodestar VP-TAE (c/n 1954) inaugurating a daily service from Trinidad-Barbados, and thrice weekly service from Trinidad-Tobago. Several Lockheed twin types were bought to expand services through-

out the Windward and Leeward Islands, adding new routes to Grenada, Jamaica and British Guiana.

In August 1947, British South American Airways Corporation (BSAAC) bought 47% of BWIA shares followed, on 1st October, when another 28% was acquired by BSAAC's subsidiary British International Airlines (BIA). BSAAC now owned 75% of shares and, with control, combined BIA and BWIA operations. BWIA's first Short Sealand operated trials in the Grenadines, with services to Bequia

Lockheed Lodestar model 18-56 VP-TAP (c/n 18-2319) basks in the Caribbean sunshine in 1948.

1949~1967

Vickers Viking V657/1 VP-TAT (c/n 119) 'Trinidad' in the early BWIA light blue livery at Hurn in early 1948.

and Carriacou but these were unsuccessful and the Sealands were rejected.

BIA operated BWIA services up to the 24th June 1948 when a new reconstituted BWIA was formed with $3million capital. The airline expanded and a fleet of eight Vikings were bought from British European Airways Corporation (BEAC) to replace the Lodestars.

When BSAAC merged with BOAC on the 30th July 1949 (Airways Corporation Act 1949), BWIA became a subsidiary of BOAC. In October BWIA bought a small Jamaican airline, British Caribbean Airways (BCA), which operated Kingston-Montego Bay, Kingston-Miami and Kingston-Nassau with two Douglas C-47A Dakotas but these services were integrated with BWIA's and the two Dakotas sold to Bahamas Airways.

BWIA operated eight Vickers-Armstrong Vikings between 1948-1957 until they were replaced by Vickers Viscounts from 1955. Viking V.657/1 VP-TAX (c/n 112) 'Barbados' is seen wearing the later BWIA livery. The aircraft was sold to the BOAC subsidiary British International Air Lines in 1955 as G-AGRU and leased to the Kuwait Oil Company.

1949~1967

BWIA operated Viscounts between Bermuda and New York in association with BOAC from 1st January 1956. Here we see Vickers-Armstrong's V.722 Viscount VP-TBS (c/n 235) in a smart combined BWIA/BOAC livery at JFK, New York City in 1958.

In 1952 BWIA operated Bahamas Airways' routes from Nassau to Miami, and to Havana with Vikings. New routes were added from Trinidad to Guadeloupe, Haiti and Puerto Rico and four Vickers-Armstrong V.702 Viscounts, the first turbo-propeller airliners registered in the Caribbean, were introduced between December 1955 and March 1956 to replace the sturdy Vikings which were then sold. The

Viscounts operated twice weekly from Trinidad-Barbados-Puerto Rico and Trinidad-Caracus-Kingston, bringing new standards of comfort and speed to the region. From July 1955, BWIA managed British Guiana Airways Ltd. for the Guianan Government, and their BWIA Viscounts also operated BOAC services from Kingston-Montego Bay-Nassau and Nassau-Miami from December 1955 and

BOAC-owned Viscount V.702 9Y-TBN (c/n 81) was leased to BWIA in November 1955 for a period of ten years, then later leased to Bahamas Airways for a further year as VP-BCI. Here it is seen at Kingston, Jamaica on 15th October 1965.

1949~1967

Boeing 727-78 9Y-TCO (c/n 18794) was operated by BWIA from December 1964 until June 1971,
when it was sold to Braniff International Airlines as N305BN.

for the Trinidad-Miami service in January 1965 and also leased an Aer Lingus Boeing 720-048 for six months in December 1966 which operated to New York.

The Government of Trinidad acquired 90% of

BWIA shares from BOAC Associated Companies on 1st November 1961. Six years later, in 1967, BOAC Associated Companies sold the last 10% of BWIA shares, again to the Government of Trinidad, selling a total of 2,500 shares valued at TT$50 (Trinidad and Tobago dollars).

BOAC operated BWIA's trans-atlantic services from 29th April 1960, visiting London-New York-Barbados-Trinidad.
As can be seen in this photo, the Britannia 312 aircraft used, in this case G-AOVL (c/n 13418),
flew with the standard livery with BWIA stickers applied to the fuselage top.

1955~1963

Grumman G.21A Goose VP-GAC (c/n B46 / BuA 37793) VP-GAC.

Mr. Arthur 'Art' James Williams formed British Guiana Airways Ltd. (BGA) during 1939 in Georgetown, British Guiana and signed a three year agreement on the 30th June with the Government of Guiana to provide pilot training, local air services and aircraft maintenance. He operated a small single-engine Ireland N-2A amphibian flying boat (c/n 47), registered NC183M (later VP-GAE) manufactured by Mr. G. S. Ireland at Curtiss Field, USA. Williams became a Major in the U.S. Army based at Atkinson Field and operated rescue missions for downed pilots for which he gained the 'Air Medal'. He returned to BGA and in June 1944 inaugurated services from Georgetown to Tumerang, later to Imbaimadai (fortnightly) and Georgetown-Letham or Janari, and to Wichabai and Lumid Pau (monthly).

When BWIA opened a service from Port of Spain, Trinidad to Georgetown in September 1945,

BGA was contracted to provide the service from Mackenzie City to Georgetown by a Goose. BGA bought a second Goose and two Douglas DC-3s in November 1946 and within two years had developed a network of domestic routes in the islands. In 1948 the airline operated Grumman Goose amphibians for British West Indian Airways from Georgetown-Port of Spain-St. Vincent, extended to Dominica in 1950, and also operated from a base on St. Vincent, Grenada and Barbados during 1951. By 1952 BGA had three Douglas DC-3s and three Goose amphibians.

In July 1955 the Government of Guiana bought BGA from Williams and arranged for BWIA to manage the airline until 1963 when the country gained independence from the United Kingdom and BGA was then renamed Guyana Airlines.

Beechcraft D.50 Twin Bonanza VP-LIF (c/n DH297) taken in Antigua on 27th December 1965.

LIAT 1956~1967

DH.114 Heron 2 VP-LIB (c/n 14082) seen wearing the attractive livery of LIAT at Antigua on 17th April 1965.

Frank de Lisle, the manager of a banana plantation on Montserrat, suffered from seasickness and he found the regular 35 mile boat ride to Antigua, taking 6 hours, to be unbearable, so he decided to learn to fly and in 1955 bought a Piper Apache aircraft which he kept on his plantation.

In 1956, he formed Leeward Islands Air Transport Ltd. (LIAT) with assistance from B.W.I.A. (wholly owned by BOAC) who acquired 75% of his shares. Services were then operated from Montserrat to Antigua, Anguilla, Guadeloupe, Puerto Rico and St Kitts with a twin-engine Piper Apache which carried three passengers. The company then expanded with four Twin Bonanzas, two de Havilland Herons and a DC-3C, with the main base then established at Coolidge Airport, Antigua.

In early 1965, the Avro 748 demonstrator G-ARMV (as VP-LII) was leased for four months until LIAT's first 748, VP-LIK fitted with 48 seats, arrived in April 1965. This was followed by the second 748 in March 1966, at which point the Herons were returned to BWIA. The 748 turboprops brought new standards of comfort and speed to LIAT and, because of increasing traffic, it was found necessary to lease a number of HS 748s for short periods over several years. Two DHC-6 Twin Otters were also delivered during 1967 for use on services to some of the smaller islands.

The Trinidad Government bought 90% of the BWIA shares from BOAC on 1st November 1961 and the remaining 10% in 1966-1967, ending B.O.A.C.'s involvement with the airline.

LIAT DC-3C VP-LIL (c/n 13114) sitting idle on the grass at Antigua on 27th December 1965.

1941~1974

TCA Avro 691 Lancastrian CF-CMW prepares to land in the UK after another North Atlantic crossing.

Trans-Canada Air Lines (TCA) was formed on the 10th April 1937 by an Act of Parliament and a service from Vancouver to Seattle was inaugurated on 1st September 1937 with twin-engine Lockheed Model 10A Electras. By 1939 TCA's fleet had increased to five Electras and nine Model 14 Super Electras which carried BOAC's 'Speedbird' logo.

BOAC's relationship with TCA began on 4th May 1941 when BOAC pilots and management, under the Atlantic Ferry Organisation, inaugurated the North Atlantic Return Ferry Service (RFS) from St Hubert, Montreal-Squires Gate, Blackpool with Liberator LB-30As. The service later operated from Dorval, Montreal-Prestwick, Scotland and TCA supplied some aircrew and serviced the Liberators at Dorval where

Bristol 170 Freighter CF-TFX (c/n 13137) prepares to land during a test flight from Filton.

1941~1974

DC-4M2 CF-TFB (c/n 126) 'Cornwallis' in flight over Canada in 1947.

BOAC built up the main RFS base. BOAC became fully responsible for the RFS service on 24th September 1941.

A British built Avro Lancaster Mk.III (Serial R5727) CF-CMS was modified to carry mail/freight, and fitted with ten forward facing seats, becoming known as the Lancaster Airmail. This was followed on the 22nd/23rd July 1943, when the Canadian Government's Trans-Atlantic Air Service (CGTAS) began to be operated by TCA's Airmail from Dorval to Prestwick, in a record time of 12hrs 26mins. Two Canadian X Lancasters were modified to Lancaster X Transports, with faired noses and extended tail cones, followed by six more as Lancaster XPPs (Mk.X Passenger Plane) with elongated nose and tail cones. Avro were impressed with the XPPs and built 82 similar Avro 691 Lancastrians for the British and worldwide market.

1049G Super Connie CF-TGE (c/n 4544) taxies at Vancouver in November 1959.

1941~1974

Trans-Canada Airlines had a substantial fleet of fifteen V.724 and 36 Series V.757 Viscounts. Here we see CF-TID (c/n 384), fleet no. 648, after landing at Seattle in July 1962.

In 1945, TCA acquired 27 DC-3s to replace the Lockheed Twin Electras and to expand domestic and North American routes. On 15th/16th September 1946, the CGTAS was extended to Heathrow and, by the year end, had flown 1,000 trips using Lancasters. These were replaced on 15th April 1947, initially by DC-4M unpressurised North Stars with 40 passenger seats from Montreal-Sydney (Nova Scotia)-London, then later also via Shannon and Montreal-Sydney-Prestwick.

On 1st May, the airline formed TCA (Atlantic) Ltd. as they had been given the task to operate the CGTAS on a commercial footing. BOAC ordered 22 pressurised C-4 'North Stars' powered by Rolls Royce Merlin Engines to replace the cancelled Avro Tudors. The North Stars inaugurated the Montreal-Bermuda and Toronto-Bermuda routes in May 1948, and later to the Caribbean from Montreal-Toronto-Nassau-Kingston-Port of Spain on 2nd December and then Barbados in 1949.

A partial Air Service Agreement was signed by TCA and BOAC in 1949. Three Bristol Mk.31 freighters were bought in October 1953 for cargo operations but were sold to Central Northern Airways in December 1955.

TCA Douglas DC-8-41 CF-TJB (c/n 45443) awaits passengers in July 1960.

1941~1974

The first of TCA's 23 Vickers-Armstrong V.952 Vanguards CF-TKA (c/n 724), fleet no. 901, during an early test flight before delivery to the airline in November 1961.

TCA replaced the faithful North Stars on the North Atlantic routes with Super Constellations from 14th May 1954 and the following year introduced fifteen turboprop V.724 Viscounts in North America, from Montreal to Winnipeg on 1st April 1955, and three days later from Toronto to New York. They were a phenomenal success and took the continent by storm, so 36 improved series V.757s were introduced into service over the following years. TCA and BOAC agreed a pool partnership for Canadian-UK services operated with BOAC Comet 4s and TCA Super Connies from 1st March 1960.

TCA's first jet, the Douglas DC-8-41 powered by Rolls Royce Conways, introduced 'Jetliner Services' on 1st April 1960 from Montreal-Toronto-Vancouver, and on 1st June from Montreal to London along with BOAC Boeing 707s. TCA bought 23 Vickers Vanguards powered by Rolls Royce Tyne turboprops which were introduced on 1st February 1961 on the Montreal-Toronto-Winnipeg-Regina-Calgary-Vancouver route, then in April to the

Caribbean and in June to New York. The older aircraft were gradually retired; the North Stars in 1961, Super Constellations in 1962 and DC-3s in 1963, the year in which TCA began to operate DC-8-54F passenger/ freighters to London.

On 1st June 1964 the company was renamed Air Canada and two years later in 1966, BOAC replaced some of their Boeing 707 services to Canada with Super VC10s, whilst TCA continued to expand with additional DC-8s. Also in 1966, DC-9s were introduced to replace the Viscounts which were being phased out.

BOAC and Air Canada joined forces to build their own passenger terminal at JFK which they then shared with BWIA and Qantas, and this was officially opened by HRH Princess Alexandra on 24th September 1970. In 1971, Air Canada introduced three B747-133s to replace the DC-8s on routes to Europe followed in 1973 when eight Tristar 1s were introduced on the North American routes. The pool partnership continued with BA from 1974.

Air Canada Douglas DC-9-10 CF-TLD (c/n 0000) at Toronto in May 1966.

1946~1967

DH.104 Dove Srs. 1 VP-YHU (c/n 04132) 'Weaver' taken at Hatfield before delivery in 1948.

On 13th October 1933, Imperial Airways (Africa) Ltd. and the Beit Railway Trust Ltd. formed Rhodesia and Nyasaland Airways Ltd. (RANA) with capital of £25,500 and took over the Rhodesian Aviation Co. Ltd. Services were operated by four de Havilland Puss Moths from Salisbury to Johannesburg and in 1934 from Salisbury to Blantyre. RANA then leased a three-engined Westland Wessex G-ABEG from Imperial Airways and this was used on a weekly service from Blantyre-Salisbury-Bulawayo-Livingstone-Lusaka-Broken Hill-Ndola. More de Havilland types joined the fleet; a single-engine Fox Moth, Leopard Moths, and twin-engine Rapides. In November 1935, the first of five Rapides (five seats) replaced the Wessex (four seats) on scheduled services. Unfortunately the Wessex had to make a forced landing at Chirindu in Northern Rhodesia the following year and consequently was written off.

At the end of 1936 the first de Havilland Dragonfly entered service and Imperial Airways replaced the Atalanta landplane on the African trunk route with Short 'C' class flying-boats in June 1937. These diverted from the old route at Kisumu and followed the east coast via Mombassa, Dar es Salaam, and Beira to Durban. RANA also opened two new routes; from Lusaka-Blantyre-Salisbury-Beira and from Johannesburg-Pietersburg-Bulawayo-Salisbury-Beira to connect with the new service between the UK and Durban.

Britain declared war on Germany in September 1939 and, on 1st February 1940, it was agreed that

Bristol 170 Mk.21E Freighter VP-YHW (c/n 12779) sits in typical grass field operating conditions in Africa in 1949.

1946~1967

CAA operated twelve Vickers Vikings during twelve years of service between 1947 and 1959 and, during 1951, the aircraft operated eleven weekly 'Inter-City' link services between Salisbury and Bulawayo. Viking V.614/1A YP-YHJ (c/n 139) 'Sabi' takes a test flight before delivery to the airline in 1947.

RANA's assets and aircraft would be acquired by the Government of Southern Rhodesia for £20,000 to form the Southern Rhodesian Air Services (SRAS) based at Belvedere Air Station, Salisbury as part of the Rhodesian Air Force to operate communication services in Central Africa.

After the end of WWII, the Central African Airways Corporation (CAA) was formed in Salisbury on 1st June 1946 by the Governments of Northern Rhodesia (35% stock), Southern Rhodesia (50%) and Nyasaland (15%). The airline inherited five Avro Ansons, one de Havilland DH.82A Tiger Moth, one DH.85 Leopard Moth and thirteen DH.89A Rapides from SRAS. CAA then made a bold decision and ordered Doves and Vikings for delivery in October/November 1946, but the airline was soon losing money and

DH.104 Dove 1 VP-YES (c/n 04006) 'Lourie' and V.616/1A Viking VP-YEW (c/n 146) 'Zambezi' prepare for delivery to the airline during 1946.

1949~1967

Douglas C-47B 9Y-TBJ (c/n 33189/16441) 'Tobago' at Piarco Airport, Port-of-Spain, Trinidad on 10th April 1966.

Bermuda-New York in January 1956.

In late 1956 BWIA formed British Honduras Airways (BHA) from British Colonial Airlines in Belize with two Cessna 180s for charter. BWIA also began trans-atlantic operations with wet leased BOAC Britannia 312s on 29th April 1960 from Trinidad-Barbados-New York-London and, on 11th December from Trinidad-Barbados-Antigua-

Bermuda-New York. The BOAC Britannias also supplemented BWIA Viscounts on the busy winter service from Jamaica to Miami from 22nd January 1961 until 1962 when they were replaced by Boeing 707-436s.

A BOAC/BWIA partnership was formed in June 1961 and leased BOAC Boeing 707s operated from Trinidad to London. BWIA added three Boeing 727-78s

BOAC Boeing 707-436 G-APFE (c/n 17706) wears BWIA stickers at Heathrow Airport on 8th September 1962 for the service to Montego Bay.

1946~1967

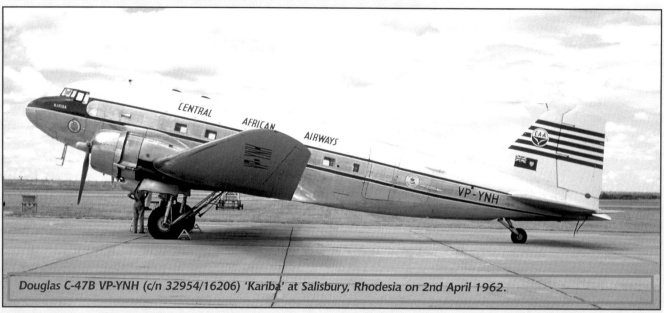

Douglas C-47B VP-YNH (c/n 32954/16206) 'Kariba' at Salisbury, Rhodesia on 2nd April 1962.

BOAC was invited to audit the company. Their report was submitted in December and so began the long-term BOAC/CAA relationship. Vikings were introduced on the 19th November operating the main South-North trade route from Johannesburg-Salisbury-Nairobi, whilst the Doves operated services from Salisbury to Blantyre and Salisbury to Bulawayo from the 9th December. CAA also leased two Bristol B.170 Mk. 21E Freighters configured as passenger-cum-freighters with 32 removable seats and an adjustable bulkhead. The first VP-YHW arrived on 2nd August 1948 and inaugurated the 'Copper Trader' service on 16th August from Lusaka-Salisbury and also Ndola-Lusaka-Bulawayo-Johannesburg. The second B.170 VP-YHZ arrived in October but both aircraft left in December 1949 to join the West African Airways Corporation (WAAC) of Lagos.

On 1st April 1950 the Golden Viking direct service was introduced from Salisbury-Johannesburg, and also a service from Salisbury-Blantyre-Dar es Salaam-Nairobi. Then, on 1st January 1951, rugged DHC.2 Beavers were introduced in the rural areas of Southern Rhodesia connecting Fort Victoria, Gatooma, Gwelo, Que Que and Umtali to Salisbury and Bulawayo. More Vikings arrived and operated from Salisbury-Livingstone (Victoria Falls) on 25th March, Johannesburg-Livingstone on 1st April, 'Starlight' low fare night flights from Salisbury-Bulawayo-Johannesburg on 1st July, and also Salisbury-Bulawayo-Lourenço Marques on 10th August. The Beavers were a great success so more were bought and on 1st December they started services in Northern Rhodesia and Nyasaland.

During September 1952, a meeting took place in

DC-6 I-DIMT (c/n 43217) is seen at Salisbury on 6th January 1963 whilst under lease from Alitalia.

1946~1967

Viscount V.748 VP-YNA (c/n 98) 'Malvern' at Blantyre, Nyasaland (now Malawi) in 1956.

London between BOAC, their Springbok partner SAA and CAA at the request of the Southern Africa Air Transport Council to look at future plans, especially new tourist routes. CAA joined the pool partnership and agreed to operate the Zambezi Colonial Coach Service with Vikings from Salisbury to London which began on 3rd April 1953 operated by 'Sabi' (see photo pg 85) taking only four days! The same month CAA received the first of eight DC-3s which

increased the capacity on national and rural services. On 26th June, UK airlines Hunting Air Transport and Airwork also flew coach services with Vikings from London to Salisbury via Nice-Malta-Mersa-Matruh-Wadi Halfa-Khartoum-Juba-Entebbe-Tabora-Ndola-Lusaka.

CAA then ordered five Viscounts and the first turboprop was delivered at Wisley, England on the

From 1st January 1951, five passenger de Havilland Canada DHC.2 Beavers replaced Doves in service to smaller destinations and proved very successful. Here in April 1963, Beaver VP-YHH (c/n 122) 'Eland' displays the airline's full colours.

1946~1967

DC-3 7Q-YKM of Air Malawi seen at Salisbury, Rhodesia preparing for the return journey to Blantyre, Malawi.

25th April 1956, starting operations on 1st June from Salisbury to Blantyre, Durban, Johannesburg, Lusaka, Ndola and Nairobi.

On the 1st July 1956, CAA agreed to operate a weekly Springbok service to London in partnership with BOAC and SAA. BOAC and CAA then signed a ten year agreement in May 1957 to fly services to London for a guaranteed £1.34 million profit. BOAC's newest aircraft, the Britannia 102, flew the CAA services from Salisbury to London in July, but these were replaced with the Britannia 312 on 31st July 1958. Then, in August, the Zambezi Coach Vikings to London were replaced with the faster Viscounts, as were all Viking services by January 1959. CAA were innovative and introduced 'Skycoast' all-inclusive holidays to Durban on the Natal coast as well as 'Skycruise', a flight to Durban and a Union Castle Line cruise along the coast to Cape Town for the return flight.

BOAC replaced Britannias with the 'Rhodesian Comet' services to London starting on 2nd December 1959 and an Alitalia Douglas DC-6 was

Air Rhodesia DC-3 VP-YNH taxies in at Salisbury, March 1972.

1946~1967

Zambia Airways DC-3 VP-YKH sits idle at Salisbury, Rhodesia on 21st March 1964.

leased for three years in January 1963 for long-haul charters. A Quadripartite Partnership between BOAC, CAA, EAA and SAA was signed on 1st October 1960 to pool services to Europe and across Africa but, despite being very successful, it was terminated three years later on 12th October 1963 for political reasons.

On 4th December 1963 the three Governments of Nyasaland, Northern and Southern Rhodesia signed an agreement to form their own airlines. In 1964 Britain granted independence to Nyasaland, which became Malawi, and Northern Rhodesia became Zambia. Southern Rhodesia was not granted independence until 1980 when it

became Zimbabwe, but it did form Air Rhodesia (Pvt) in June 1964. Their respective airlines - Air Malawi (formed in March 1964), Zambia Airways Ltd. (April) and Air Rhodesia (June) were established as subsidiaries of CAA and the fleet was split up. The Beavers went to Air Malawi and Zambia Airways whilst the DC-3s were shared between all three airlines. CAA continued operations with the Viscounts linking the three countries and also flying regional routes to surrounding countries until 31st December 1967 when CAA was dissolved because of political unrest in Rhodesia. The Viscounts were passed to Air Rhodesia and Air Malawi, and the two BAC 1-11s to Zambia Airways.

BAC 1-11-207AJ 9J-RCI (c/n 040) taken at London's Heathrow Airport awaiting delivery to British Eagle Airways who leased the aircraft for a period of eleven months.

1946~1969

DH.89A Dragon Rapide VP-KCJ (c/n 6366) in an idle moment in 1947.

The East African Airways Corporation (EAAC) was formed on the 1st January 1946 by the Governments of Kenya, Tanganyika, Uganda and Zanzibar with initial capital of £50,000; 67.7% from Kenya; 22.6% from Uganda; 9% from Tanganyika and 0.7% from Zanzibar. The airline's HQ was Shell House, Delamere Avenue, Nairobi and the main base at Eastleigh Aerodrome, Nairobi.

As Technical Adviser to EAAC, BOAC operated their trunk routes, providing pilots, engineers and technical experts, and flights began on 1st January 1946 with six ex-RAF DH.89A Rapides flown by twelve ex-RAF pilots. Services operated weekly from Nairobi-Eldoret-Kitale

and from Dar es Salaam-Morogoro-Nduli-Southern Highlands-Chunya-Mbeya, twice weekly from Nairobi-Moshi-Dar es Salaam and Nairobi-Kisumu-Entebbe, three times per week from Dar es Salaam-Zanzibar-Tanga-Mombassa and five times per week from Nairobi-Mombasa-Tanga-Zanzibar-Dar es Salaam.

In 1946, an ex-Wilson Airways' Rapide was bought by EAA with a further six purchased in 1947. The following year BOAC sold EAA five Lodestar 18-56s from Almaza, Egypt with a complete spares package for only £30,000. These were delivered from 22nd February 1948 and entered service on 21st March 1948 from Nairobi to Dar er Salaam.

Lockheed 18-56 Lodestar VP-KHW (c/n 18-2035) 'Tanga Safari' at Nairobi West Airport in June 1952.

1946~1969

Canadair C4 VP-KOJ (c/n 159), ex G-ALHM 'Antaeus', taken at Heathrow in 1960.

Meanwhile the first of four new de Havilland Dove Srs.1 aircraft also arrived in February 1948 entering service on 14th April from Nairobi to Mombassa. The powerful Lodestars performed well in the African heat and high altitude so additional Lodestar 18-56s were bought from Sabena in June 1948 then, in 1950, seven Lodestar 18-08s were purchased from SAA and were modified by EAA to the more powerful 18-56s. Two ex-BOAC DC-3s arrived in 1949/50 to provide services from Nairobi-Dar es Salaam-Mozambique-Lourenço Marques-Durban and Nairobi-Mbeya-Salisbury. BOAC Solents also flew via Port Bell to Johannesburg three times per week from May 1948 and a weekly UK-Dar es Salaam service from 23rd February 1949 until they were replaced in September 1950 by Hermes aircraft.

In 1952, HRHs Princess Elizabeth and Prince Philip were visiting East Africa when they were informed of the death of King George VI. The new Queen returned home on 6th February, flying from Nanyuki to Entebbe by EAA DC-3 VP-KHK (ex-BOAC G-AGKI) and then to London by BOAC Argonaut 'Atalanta' G-ALHK. BOAC introduced Comet 1s on 2nd May 1952 to provide a service from the UK to South Africa via Entebbe whilst EAAC replaced the Lodestars with a further 9 DC-3s during 1952/53. EAA aircraft were always available and provided transportation and support for filming including 'King Solomon's Mines', 'The African Queen' and 'Mocambo' in the early 1950s. For the last film, Catalina VP-KKJ, once owned by Cathay, flew workers and supplies to a nearby river, and a bush airfield was constructed close to the Mocambo village for DC-3 operations.

Douglas C-47B Dakota 4 5X-AAS (c/n 32656/15908) taken at Nairobi on 2nd May 1964.

1946~1969

BOAC Britannia 102 G-ANBN (c/n 12915) wears EAAC stickers during 1958.

In late 1952 EAA registered the subsidiary company Seychelles-Kilimanjaro Air Transport (SKAT), with the intention of Catalina VP-KKJ, previously owned by Cathay Pacific, operating services from East Africa to the Seychelles. However the Catalina was sold in 1954 along with several Dragon Rapides, four Doves and the remaining Lodestars because a large fleet of Douglas DC-3s had been purchased. Three twin-engine Macchi 320s were also bought but they suffered persistent problems and were sold locally. An ex-BSAAC/BOAC Airspeed A.S.65 Consul G-AIUX, re-registered as VP-KMI, was also bought for flight training in 1954.

A partnership agreement was signed in 1956 with BOAC and the following year four BOAC Argonauts were leased to operate EAA trunk routes; Nairobi-

Entebbe-Khartoum-Benghazi-Rome-London starting on 2nd April, Nairobi-Dar es Salaam-Salisbury-Durban on 14th April, and Nairobi-Aden-Karachi-Bombay on 15th September in pool with Air India. When the new Nairobi International Airport opened at Embakasi on 9th March 1958, EAA built new hangars and workshops and started transferring their operations from Wilson Aerodrome.

The Argonauts could not compete with BOAC's turboprop Britannias on the Nairobi to London service, so EAA leased BOAC and British & Commonwealth Britannias from 8th October 1958 to 1961. In 1960 EAA reactivated Seychelles Kilimanjaro Air Transport and the last two EAA Rapides, VP-KEF and VP-KNS, were transferred to operate a daily service from Dar es Salaam-Zanzibar-Pemba Island-Tanga, twice weekly

Fokker F-27 Friendship 5Y-AAB (c/n 10211) seen at Embakasi in April 1964 wearing the early EAA livery.

1946~1969

The elegant form of Comet 4 5Y-AAA (c/n 6472) at Nairobi Embakasi in April 1964.

from Dar es Salaam-Kilwa, and thrice weekly from Dar es Salaam-Mafia Island.

EAA initially ordered two Comet 4s and on the 17th September 1960 began a twice weekly service from London-Rome-Khartoum-Entebbe-Nairobi, which was later extended to Dar es Salaam and to Johannesburg. With the arrival of a third Comet, daily services operated to London and twice weekly to Karachi, Bombay and also Johannesburg.

A Quadripartite partnership of BOAC, CAA, EAA and SAA was signed on 1st October 1960 to pool services within Africa and to Europe, however this agreement ended on 12th October 1963 because of political difficulties in Southern Rhodesia and EAA stopped flying to South Africa. BOAC then negotiated a new five year agreement to fly via East Africa to Johannesburg and

leased a DC-7F to EAA for their weekly London-Nairobi freight service from October 1963.

The four East African countries gained independence between 1961 and 1963, and in January 1964 Tanganyika and Zanzibar merged to form Tanzania and a new EAA livery appeared on their aircraft in 1965. BOAC Comet G-APDL was leased from October 1965 to March 1967, whilst five Super VC10s were leased from Vickers. The first, 5X-UVA received on 30th September 1966, replaced the Comets which were transferred over time to SKAT for long-haul charters. In 1966/67 EAA repaid BOAC-AC £250,000 for the 3.5% stock.

EAA operations ceased in January 1977 when the airline went into liquidation, having incurred debts of US$120,000,000.

Douglas C-47B 5H-AAK (c/n 25815/14370) sits at Nairobi during September 1972.

1946~1969

Above:
The colourful Super VC10
5X-UVA (c/n 881) on a test
flight before delivery to
East African Airways on
30th September 1966.
Left:
De Havilland Canada DHC-6
Twin Otter 5H-MNK
(c/n NBR-40) on delivery
through Heathrow on the
15th July 1967.
Below:
De Havilland Comet 4
5H-AAF (c/n 6433) at
Heathrow on
12th November 1965.

1958~1971

Britannia 102 G-ANBK (c/n 12912) at Heathrow engineering on 3rd July 1960.

A British colony, known as the Gold Coast since 1874, became independent on 6th March 1957 and was renamed Ghana. Air services had been operated by BOAC and the West African Airways Corporation (WAAC) but on 4th July 1958 Ghana Airways Ltd. was incorporated in Accra with £400,000 capital - BOAC Associated Companies Ltd. subscribing 40% and the Government of Ghana 60%. A seven year pool agreement was also signed with BOAC to operate a service from London-Ghana using chartered BOAC aircraft with Ghana Airways' titles.

A weekly service from Accra-London was inaugurated on 15th July 1958 using a Boeing 377 Stratocruiser, G-ANTZ 'Cordelia', with mixed first and tourist-class configura-tion. The airline's relationship with West African Airways ended on 30th September and, on 1st October, Ghana Airways began to operate the internal routes previously operated by WAAC. With two new de Havilland Herons, registered 9G-AAA and 9G-AAB, delivered in December 1958 and January 1959 respectively, followed by a Douglas C-47A 9G-AAC on 9th March, Ghana Airways operated internal services to Kumasi, Takoradi and Tamale, and an international service from Accra-Freetown-Conakry-Bathurst-Dakar.

The last scheduled service by a BOAC Stratocruiser was the weekly Ghana Airways' service from Accra-Kano-Barcelona-London on 31st May 1959 by G-ANTY 'Coriolanus'. This service was

BOAC Comet 4 G-APDA (c/n 6401) with the temporary name of 'Osagyefo' (Redeemer). It was used for Prime Minister Dr. Kwame Nkrumah's state visit to the USA in March 1961.

1958~1971

Britannia 309 9G-AAG (c/n 12924) testing her engines at Filton in February 1960.

replaced with a chartered BOAC turboprop Britannia Series 102 on 14th April 1959. Ghana Airways were impressed with the Britannia and ordered two of the larger long-range 309 Series for the London-Accra route, followed by an order on 20th April for three Viscount V.838s for the Accra-Dakar route, with maintenance contracted to BOAC at Heathrow.

The airline became more independently minded and futher expanded with a fleet of Russian Ilyushin IL-18s in December 1960, joined later by an Antonov AN-12 freighter. The Russian aircraft opened many new routes but as they had to return to Moscow for servicing, they were under-utilised and several were eventually returned to the USSR in 1963.

BOAC had initially trained 24 Ghanaians as managers, pilots and engineers, but this had increased to

200 by the end of 1961 when three Viscounts were introduced to fly Accra-Abidjan-Freetown-Bathurst-Dakar and Accra-Lome-Cotonou-Lagos whilst the Herons were withdrawn and transferred to the Ghana Air Force. On 14th February 1961, the Ghanaian Government purchased BOAC's 40% shareholding.

BOAC decided to terminate the pool partnership on 10th November 1962 as the airline was unhappy with Ghana Airways' negotiations with Swissair. The airline returned a leased Britannia which was replaced with a Swissair Convair 990A Coronado for the Accra-London service in 1964/65 but then decided to purchase two VC10s in 1965 to replace the Britannia, Coronado and last remaining IL-18s, with the VC10s being maintained by BOAC at Heathrow. All BOAC commercial agreements with Ghana Airways were finally terminated on 31st March 1971.

Ilyushin IL-18V 9G-AAX (c/n 181002803) on a rare visit to Heathrow in 1962.

1958~1971

Ghana Airways' de Havilland DH.114 Heron 2D 9G-AAB (c/n 14134) sports the airline's exotic first livery at Accra on 7th June 1959.

Viscount V.838 9G-AAV (c/n 371) starts her engines for the first time at Hurn in September 1961.

Antonov AN-12BP 9G-AAZ (c/n 024009) at Gatwick in April 1962

1958~1971

Douglas C-47A Dakota III 9G-AAE (c/n 12054) at Heathrow in June 1963. Previously operated by BOAC in World War II and registered G-AGJZ, the aircraft was transferred to the British European Airways Corporation and named 'John Stringfellow' on the 1st August 1946.

Hawker Siddeley HS.748 Series 214 G-ATAM (c/n 1576) at Woodford in December 1971 wearing Ghana Airways' livery and allocated registration 9G-ABV for lease which was later cancelled. Two new HS.748s were delivered to Ghana in December 1970 and January 1971.

Convair CV-990 HB-ICA (c/n 30-10-7) wears stickers at Heathrow Airport whilst under lease from Swissair.

1967~1974

Boeing 707-465 G-ARWD (c/n 18372) 'City of Port Louis' taxies at Heathrow on 26th June 1979.

It was on 6th January 1962 that BOAC inaugurated its first weekly service with Britannia 102s to Mauritius, flying London-Rome-Khartoum-Nairobi-Mauritius taking 24 hours.

Air Mauritius was formed on the 1st June 1967 with BOAC Associated Companies and Air France holding 15% each, the Government of Mauritius 52.5%, and local Mauritian business Rogers and Company 17.5%. Air Mauritius signed a five year service agreement with BOAC and Air France for ticketing and ground handling services at Plaisance Airport, Port Louis, Mauritius.

The company restricted its activities to ground ser-

vices until August 1972 when it started operations with a six-seater Piper PA-31 Navajo 5R-MCW (c/n 31-469) leased from Air Madagascar. This inaugurated a service connecting Mauritius with Rodrigues Island 350 miles to the east across the Indian Ocean - a flight for the brave but well within legal limits.

In 1971 Air Mauritius chartered Air France aircraft capacity between Mauritius-Reunion, followed in 1972 with services from Mauritius to East Africa and Europe. A joint service from Mauritius-India began in 1973 with Air India followed by a London-Nairobi-Mauritius service when a Super VC10 was leased from BOAC. In 1974 British Airways Associated Companies owned 20% of Air Mauritius.

Standard VC10 9G-ABO (c/n 823) on a test flight from Wisley during November 1964, prior to delivery to the airline.

1945~1974

Avro York ZS-ATR (c/n 1222) 'Impala' was leased from BOAC for an eighteen month period starting January 1946.

Vickers-Armstrong's V.635/1B Viking ZS-BNL (c/n 297) 'Mount Prospect'.

BOAC Comet 1 G-ALYY (c/n 06011) taken at Heathrow in October 1953. Whilst under lease to SAA, the aircraft crashed on 8th April 1954 near Naples, Italy.

1945~1974

749A Constellation ZS-DBR (c/n 2623) 'Cape Town' taken at Johannesburg on 21st November 1962.

Major Allister M. Miller D.S.O., O.B.E. formed Union Airways (Pty) Ltd. on 24th July 1929 with five DH Gipsy Moths. He received a Government subsidy to carry mail from Port Elisabeth (his base), Johannesburg and Durban to Cape Town where the mail boats called, and the inaugural flight took place on the 26th August from Cape Town to Port Elisabeth. The airline expanded and three Junkers F 13s, a Junkers W 34 and a Fokker Universal were purchased to operate daily services from Durban to Johannesburg. Around the same time South-West Africa Airlines was formed in 1930 at Windhoek with two Junkers A 50s and a single Junkers F 13 which began operating from Windhoek to Grootfontein, Keetmanshoop and Kimberley and then in 1931 to Wavis Bay.

Several years later South African Airways (SAA) was founded in Durban by the South African Railways Authority and they took over Union Airways and began operating from Durban to Johannesburg on 1st February 1934. Three Junkers JU-52/3m which were introduced on 1st November were a great success, so twelve more were added. SAA then acquired South-West Africa Airways on the 1st February 1935, and moved base to Rand Airport Germiston near Johannesburg on the 1st July. Rapid expansion took place with four Airspeed Envoys delivered in 1936 and eighteen Junkers JU 86s in 1937. World War II began in 1939 and, on 24th May 1940, SAA became part of the South African Air Force (SAAF) and accepted delivery of 28 Lodestars ordered by SAA.

C-47A ZS-BXG (c/n 12049) 'Piketberg' also taken at Johannesburg on 21st November 1962.

1945~1974

Above: SAA's first delivered DC-4 ZS-AUA (c/n 42934) named 'Tafelberg', about to take a test flight from Santa Monica, California in March 1946 before delivery to the airline.

Below: Douglas DC-4 ZS-AUA (c/n 42934) 'Tafelberg' was delivered to SAA on 25th March 1946 and is seen in SAA service at Heathrow on the 8th September 1960 carrying a revised livery.

De Havilland DH.104 Dove Mk.6 ZS-BCC (c/n 04079) 'Katberg' was delivered as a Mk.1 to SAA on 28th December 1947 and operated until 31st January 1952 when sold. The aircraft was later bought by the SAA Historic Flight and restored in the mid 1990's.

1945~1974

DC-7B ZS-DKE (c/n 44911) 'Reiger' flies over Johannesburg.

BOAC inaugurated the 'Horseshoe' route from Durban via Egypt to Australia with Short 'C' class flying-boats on 19th June 1940. On the 1st December 1944, SAA resumed civil services with six Lodestars released from the SAAF followed by another six in 1945. After WWII, SAA and BOAC became partners to operate the joint 'Springbok' service on 10th November 1945 from Palmietfontein, Johannesburg-Nairobi-Khartoum-Cairo-Tripoli-Hurn, England with Avro Yorks. SAA introduced three DC-4s on 1st May 1946 from Johannesburg to Cape Town and on 8th July supplemented the Yorks with an express service to London. Later that year they bought DC-3s and Doves for domestic services. Three more DC-4s arrived in 1947, replacing SAA's Yorks, and eight Vikings ousted the Lodestars, seven of which were

sold to EAA. BOAC exchanged their York service to South Africa on 4th May 1948 with night stopping Solent flying-boats from Southampton-Augusta-Cairo-Luxor-Khartoum-Port Bell-Victoria Falls-Vaaldam, Johannesburg until replaced with H.P. Hermes on 7th November 1950. Pressurised faster Lockheed L-749A Constellations were phased in on the 'Springbok' service from 8th May 1950, reducing the flight time to London by eight hours.

A milestone in world aviation history was the introduction of scheduled passenger jet services by BOAC with the DH.106 Comet 1 on 2nd May 1952 from London-Rome-Beirut-Khartoum-Entebbe-Livingstone-Johannesburg. The new Jan Smuts Airport, Johannesburg with

Viscount V.813 ZS-CDY (c/n 351) 'Gemsbok' at Johannesburg on 21st November 1962.

1945~1974

Boeing 727-44 ZS-SBF (c/n 19318) 'Komati' at Johannesburg on 18th May 1969.

its 10,500ft/3,200 metre runway was officially opened on 1st September 1953 and became SAA's new headquarters and maintenance base. SAA introduced a 'jetliner' service from London to Johannesburg on 4th October 1953 together with BOAC using their Comet 1s but flown by SAA crews. Unfortunately, Comet G-ALYY crashed into the sea off Naples on 8th April 1954 whilst operating a service for SAA. As this was the second Comet 1 to break up during flight in the last three months, the Comet 1s were grounded and their 'Certificates of Airworthiness' were withdrawn. BOAC brought the Canadair C-4 into service to Johannesburg whilst SAA used more Constellations until they

were replaced, on 21st April 1956, with the first of four DC-7Bs.

An additional DC-7B express service from Johannesburg-Khartoum (later Kano)-London operated by a DC-7B began on 4th December, taking 21 hours. The 'Wallaby' service across the Indian Ocean from Johannesburg-Mauritius-Cocos Islands-Perth, taking 25 hours, also began on the 27th November 1957 in pool with Qantas.

Seven turboprop Viscount 813s replaced the ageing Constellations on domestic and regional routes and opened the new 'Bosbok' service from Johannesburg to Salisbury on 24th November

Boeing 737-244 ZS-SBM (c/n 19708) 'Gamtoos' at Johannesburg on 2nd March 1970.

1945~1974

Boeing 707-344C ZS-SAI (c/n 20283) 'East London' taken at Heathrow in September 1971.

1958. BOAC then introduced Comet 4s on the 'Springbok' route on 2nd December 1959, with SAA having to wait until 15th July 1960 for their first Boeing 707-344 which entered international services to Europe on 1st October 1963 via Las Palmas in the Canaries and in 1966 via Sal, Cape Verde Islands. Boeing 727-44s came into service on 1st August 1965 and two years later, on the 29th March 1967, the trusty DC-7 service to Australia was transformed with Boeing 707s from Johannesburg-Mauritius-Perth-Sydney. Expansion continued with Boeing 737-244s delivered on 29th October 1968, and three Boeing 707-344Cs inaugurated a service to the USA in 1969, from Johannesburg-Rio de Janeiro-New York.

BOAC signed an agreement with SAA for a weekly 707 freighter service from London to Johannesburg and three HS.748 Series 2As were ordered. The first, delivered in January 1971, was immediately leased to Botswana until May, whilst the other two were introduced into service on 25th February from Johannesburg to Gaborone, and also to Francistown, Manzini and Durban. On 22nd October 1971, the first Boeing 747-244s went into service to Europe. The BOAC/SAA partnership, which had started in 1945, continued with British Airways.

HS.748 Series 2A ZS-SBV (c/n 1692) 'Etosha', March 1971.

1946~1948

Handley Page Marathon H.P.R. 1A VR-NAN (c/n 127) named 'Lagos' in 1952.

The West African Airways Corporation (WAAC) was established on 15th May 1946 following an Order-in-Council signed by HRH King George VI. Based at Lagos and with issued capital of £450,000, the airline was owned by the Governments of the British Colonies of The Gambia (0.5%), Gold Coast (29.5%) Nigeria (68%), and Sierra Leone (2%). The airline was formed to operate air services between the respective countries and also to provide domestic services in Nigeria and the Gold Coast. BOAC signed an agreement with WAAC as an associated company and seconded over 100 technical staff including air and ground crews.

During 1946 BOAC Dakotas based at Whitchurch, Bristol operated the UK to West Africa service via Lisbon-Casablanca-Bathurst-Lagos to Kano three times per week, and under the name of Nigerian Air Services operated from Lagos to Port Harcourt-Enugu-Jos-Kaduna-and Kano (873 miles/1,405 kms) for the Nigerian Government. From the 2nd July 1947, Dakotas operating the UK to Nigeria route were replaced

WAAC's first de Havilland DH.104 Dove Series 1 VR-NAB (c/n 04044) seen at Hatfield before delivery in August 1947.

1946~1948

BOAC Canadair C-4 Argonaut G-ALHY (c/n 170) 'Arion' at Heathrow with WAAC titles.

by Handley Page Haltons, with ten passenger seats, and a trans-Sahara service beginning on 1st September from London-Tripoli-Kano-Lagos-Accra brought Nigeria within 24 hours of London. On 28th October 1947, a service from Lagos to Calabar via Benin, Port Hartcourt and Enuga was inaugurated with de Havilland Doves and, by 31st March 1948, nine Doves had arrived and replaced the BOAC Dakota services in West Africa. Domestic routes were developed to Ibadan, Ilorin, Kano, Maiduguri, Potiskum, Tiko and Yola, and WAAC also flew the inter-Colonial coastal service from Lagos-Accra-Takoradi-Freetown-Bathurst-Dakar, Senegal (1,900 miles/3,058 kms), connecting with BSAA's UK-South American route.

The Haltons operating the UK-Accra route were replaced by Avro Yorks (21 seats) on 1st May 1948, operating until August 1950 when they were replaced by the H.P. 81 Hermes 4. With the arrival of two ex-CAA Bristol 170 Freighters and two 170 Wayfarers with 48 seats, weekly low fare coach services were introduced from Lagos-Benin-Port Harcourt and Lagos-Jos-Kano in November 1949, and later from Accra to Khartoum and Lagos to Dakar in April 1950. WAAC then took delivery of six H.P.

BOAC Boeing B.377-10-34 Stratocruiser G-ANUB (c/n 15969) 'Calypso', which was chartered to WAAC, is seen at Heathrow in 1958.

1946~1958

Above & Left:
De Havilland DH.114
Heron 2 VR-NCE
(c/n 14091) in
December 1955.

Bottom:
DC-3 G-AOUD
(c/n 25573/14128)
of Transair was one of
three DC-3s used during
the state visit of Queen
Elizabeth II to Nigeria in
1956.

1958~1971

DH.104 Dove 1 VR-NOB (c/n 04207) R.M.A. 'Omifunfun' taken at Gatwick on 30th March 1961.

Marathons, configured with eighteen seats, from November 1952 but they were found to be unsuitable and were returned to the UK by 1954. The Hermes were replaced on the UK-Nigeria route with a daily Argonaut service in late 1953, and WAAC ordered eight Herons which arrived from April 1955 to replace the Doves, except 'Omifunfun' which was a special aerial survey version.

A partnership agreement was signed with BOAC in 1956 to operate a weekly London-Lagos tourist flight, and later the following year BOAC operated services from the UK to Nigeria for WAAC using Argonauts which were then replaced with

Stratocruisers in 1958. The Bristol 170s were also sold and seven DC-3s acquired.

When the Gold Coast gained independence on 6th March 1957, the country became known as Ghana and formed Ghana Airways on 4th July 1958 in Accra. WAAC was dissolved on the 30th September 1958 but the following day, 1st October 1958, WAAC (Nigeria) Ltd. was formed with the Nigerian Government holding 51%, Elder-Dempster Lines Ltd. 32.5% and BOAC Associated Companies 16.5%. The airline operated as Nigeria Airways, sometimes using the title of Nigerian Airways, and a fifteen year agreement was signed with BOAC to charter their aircraft and pool services on the UK to Nigeria

DH.114 Heron 2 VR-NAW (c/n 14077) 'Ikeja' at Kano in 1959.

1958~1971

Boeing B.377-10-34 Stratocruiser G-ANTX (c/n 15965) 'Cleopatra' seen at Heathrow in 1959.

route. BOAC Stratocruisers now operated a weekly Nigeria Airways first-class service from London-Rome-Kano-Lagos and a first/tourist-class service from London-Frankfurt-Rome-Kano-Lagos until 16th April 1959 when they were replaced with Britannia 102s. The seven Nigeria Airways' Dakotas and three chartered from BEA operated the domestic service and also, in co-operation with Ghana Airways, operated a service from Lagos to Dakar.

During 1960, the Herons were phased out and sold - five to Itavia of Italy and three to Overseas Aviation of England. Nigeria then gained independence on 1st October 1960 and the Nigerian Government acquired all WAAC (Nigeria) shares held by BOAC and the Elder-Dempster Lines Ltd. in March 1961. Two small five-seat Piper PA-23 Aztec 250s were delivered in early 1961 for local services, followed by three turboprop Fokker

F.27-200s in September 1962 which operated from Lagos-Accra-Abidjan-Robertsfield-Monrovia-Freetown-Bathurst-Dakar, Lagos-Cotonou-Lome-Accra, Lagos-Port Harcourt-Calabar-Tiko, and also Lagos-Douala-Leopoldville. The BOAC Britannias were replaced in October 1962 with Nigeria Airways' first jet, the Boeing 707, used until June 1964 when VC10s took over. Nigeria Airways secured the long term operation of BOAC's VC10 G-ARVC in January 1966 and this was painted in full Nigerian livery. In March 1969 the airline added two Fokker F-27-600s, and in September they bought BOAC VC10 G-ARVA and registered it in Nigeria as 5N-ABD. The long standing agreement to operate BOAC aircraft for Nigeria Airways therefore ceased in October with all of BOAC's commercial agreements terminated by 31st March 1971.

Boeing 707-436 G-ARRA (c/n 18411) sports Nigeria Airways' stickers at Heathrow.

1958~1971

On the 28th September 1962, Bristol 175 Britannia Series 102 G-ANBK (c/n 12912) wears Nigeria Airways' stickers at London Heathrow Airport.

Right:
Douglas C-47A
Dakota 3 G-AJHZ
(c/n 12421)
seen at
Heathrow, was
leased from BEA.

Douglas DC-7C G-AOIC (c/n 45113) at Heathrow in January 1961.

1958~1971

Standard VC10 G-ARVB (c/n 805) wearing Nigeria stickers, taxies in at Geneva, Switzerland in June 1965.

Standard VC10 G-ARVC (c/n 806) at Heathrow in March 1966 whilst under an eighteen month lease from BOAC.

Standard VC10 5N-ABD (c/n 804) taken at Heathrow in October 1969 after outright purchase by Nigeria Airways.

1958~1961

One of three de Havilland DH.89A Dragon Rapide Mk.4s acquired in England by WAAC (Nigeria) Ltd. for use by Sierra Leone Airways. VR-LAE (c/n 6827) RMA 'Kassewe' was delivered in July 1958.

Sierra Leone Airways Ltd. (SLA) was founded in early 1958 by the Sierra Leone Government and was based at Leone House, Freetown as a subsidiary of WAAC (Nigeria) Ltd. Three de Havilland DH.89A Rapides were bought in England and were delivered in January (VR-LAC), in May (VR-LAD) and July 1958 (VR-LAE).

SLA operated a network of services from Lungi Airport, Freetown's international airport on the side of the Sierra Leone River estuary. A regular service was operated from Hastings Airport, fifteen miles outside of Freetown, with a fifteen minute flight to Lungi airport where services operated on to Bo, Kenema, Magburaka, Port Loko and Yengama.

Sierra Leone Airways ceased operations in January 1961 because of a negative cash flow, however the airline was resurrected in March 1961 when the Government signed a contract with British United Airways (BUA) who acquired a 70% shareholding with local interests holding the remaining 30%.

BUA decided to lease two Scottish Aviation Twin Pioneers to operate domestic services and, on international services from 16th November 1961, the BUA Britannias opened a weekly non-stop service from London to Freetown in company colours carrying Sierra Leone stickers.

Scottish Aviation Twin Pioneer Series 1 5N-ABR (c/n 526) at Blackbushe in 1961.

1962~1972

De Havilland DH.106 Comet 4 G-APDP (c/n 6417) is prepared for flight at BOAC Headquarters, Heathrow Airport in 1962.

Left:
BOAC Standard VC10 G-ARVH (c/n 810) parked at the engineering base at Heathrow on 1st May 1967, sporting the short-lived Goldline livery and Air Ceylon stickers.

VC10 G-ARVF (c/n 808) flew for Air Ceylon intermittently on lease and is seen in the final BOAC livery at Paya Lebar Airport, Singapore on 31st August 1969.

1962~1972

The sole Hawker Siddeley HS.121 Trident 1E 4R-ACN (c/n 2135) operated by Air Ceylon from July 1969.

The Air Transport Branch of Ceylon's Directorate of Civil Aviation formed Ceylon Airways in 1947. With technical support from Air India, services began on 3rd December 1947 using Douglas C-47 Dakotas from their Colombo base to Trincomalee and Jaffa, and to Madras on 10th December. Two Rapides also operated domestic routes from Colombo to Minneriya, Aparai and Trincomalee.

In 1948, the airline was renamed Air Ceylon and an agreement was signed with Australian National Airways Pty. Ltd. (ANA) in August to operate from London-Colombo-Sydney (and Trichinopoly, Madras and Karachi) with two DC-4s. Services were then inaugurated from Colombo to London and Colombo to Singapore during 1949, extending to Sydney on 28th January 1950.

By Act of Parliament, Air Ceylon was reconstituted on 1st May 1951, with the Government holding 51% stock and ANA 49%. However, with a downturn in international traffic, ANA pulled out in 1953 and the DC-4s were returned to Australia. ANA's shares were bought by KLM in October 1955.

On 1st February 1956, Air Ceylon operated from Colombo-Bombay-Karachi-Cairo-Rome-Amsterdam-London using an L-749A Constellation. This was upgraded in 1958 with an L-1049G Super Constellation which was subsequently replaced by a Lockheed Electra from 1st November 1960 to 1st November 1961 to operate the 'Sapphire' service.

BOAC signed an agreement with Air Ceylon to operate a new 'Sapphire Jet' Comet service beginning on 30th March 1962 from London-Rome-Cairo-Bahrain-Karachi-Colombo, and later to Singapore. In November 1964, Air Ceylon bought an HS.748 to replace the Dakotas (DC-3s) which were still operating from Colombo-Gal Oya-Batticaloa-Trincomalee-Jaffna, Colombo-Anuradhapura-Jaffna and Colombo-Jaffna-Madras and they also added a Nord 262A in 1967 for domestic routes.

During 1967, the BOAC Comets were replaced with VC10s, later upgraded with Super VC10s, and then, in July 1969, Air Ceylon bought an HS.121 Trident IE which operated from Colombo to Singapore and Colombo to Karachi where it was serviced by the Pakistan International Airlines Corporation. Air Ceylon terminated the agreement with BOAC on 31st March 1972.

Hawker Siddeley HS.748 Series 212 4R-ACJ (c/n 1571) was introduced into service in November 1964 replacing the Douglas DC-3 on domestic routes.

1951~1974

749 Constellation VT-CQR (c/n 2505) 'Rajput Princess' at Heathrow on 22nd March 1948. It was sold to Qantas as VH-EAE in December 1949, and then to BOAC as G-ANTG 'Bournemouth' in 1954.

In 1932 a South African aviator called Nevill Vintcent came up with an idea to run mail flights to connect with the Imperial Airways flights at Karachi. Together with Mr. J.R.D. Tata of the Aviation Department of Tata Sons Limited, they inaugurated an airmail service on 15th October 1932 using DH.80A Puss Moths from Karachi-Ahmedabad-Bombay-Bellary-Madras. This was extended in 1935 from Bombay to Trivandrum, in 1936 from Madras to Colombo and in 1937 from Bombay to Delhi, by now using two DH.83 Fox Moths, two Miles Merlins, ten Waco YQC-6s and three Rapides. The company was renamed Tata Air Lines on 22nd January 1938 and two DH.86As were purchased. Unfortunately during WWII, many Tata aircraft were requisitioned but they decided to

buy five Stinson Model As in November 1941 for a limited network and at the end of the war, in November 1945, eighteen war-surplus Dakotas were acquired. The airline was renamed Air India Ltd. and an order was placed for eight Vickers Viking IBs which were introduced from April 1947.

When India gained Independence in 1947, the country required an international flag carrier and on 8th March 1948, Air India International Ltd. (A.I.I.) was formed with the Indian Government holding 49% shares and Air-India Ltd. 51%. On 8th June 1948, A.I.I. inaugurated a Bombay-Cairo-Geneva-London service with one of three L-749 Constellations, VT-CQP 'Malabar Princess'. This route was later extended to Rome in 1950, Paris (Orly) in

749A Constellation VF-DAR (c/n 2619) 'Maratha Princess' in flight.

1951~1974

1049C Super Constellation VT-DGL (c/n 4547) 'Empress Nurjehan', April 1954

1951 and Dusseldorf in 1953. Four L-749A Constellations were added whilst two of the earlier L-749s were sold to Qantas and then later to BOAC. On 21st January 1950, L-749As operated from Bombay-Aden-Nairobi, and later via Karachi.

A full agreement was signed between A.I.I. and BOAC in April 1951. The Indian Government Air Corporation's Bill 1953 received Presidential Assent on 28th May and A.I.I. was nationalised and became Air-India International Corporation on 15th June 1953. With Mr. J.R.D. Tata as Chairman, the airline ordered five Super Constellations and two Comet 3s (although never built). The Super Connies flew to London on 19th June 1954 and replaced the L-749As which were transferred to the Bombay-Madras-Singapore

route on 16th July, the Bombay-Calcutta-Bangkok-Hong Kong route on 14th August (extended to Tokyo in May 1955), and the Bombay-Madras-Singapore-Darwin-Sydney route on 5th October 1956. A.I.I. also introduced weekly Bombay-Delhi-Tashkent-Moscow services with Super Constellations pooled with Aeroflot using Tupolev TU-104A twin-engine jets on 14th August 1958.

On 4th December 1959, a tripartite partnership was signed by BOAC, Qantas and Air India in Bombay to pool the UK-India-Australia, Hong Kong-Tokyo and London-New York services effective from 1st April 1960. This was in time for the three Boeing 707-437s delivered in February/March which inaugurated A.I.I. jet services from Bombay-Cairo-Rome-London on 19th April, extended to

1049E Super Constellation VT-DHL (c/n 4613) 'Rani of Ajanta' at Heathrow on 12th April 1957.

1951~1974

Boeing 707-437 VT-DJI (c/n 17722) 'Nandi Devi' before delivery in February 1960.

New York on 14th May. A.I.I.'s services were integrated with Qantas using short bodied 707-138s from London - Frankfurt - Rome - Cairo - Karachi-Calcutta-Bangkok-Singapore-Darwin-Brisbane-Sydney from the 27th October 1959, and BOAC's Comet 4s from London-Beirut-Karachi-Singapore-Sydney on 1st November 1959. Two L-1049Gs, modified to L-1049H convertible freighters by Lockheed Aircraft Services in California, inaugurated the 'Flying Sherpa' cargo service on 14th November 1960 from London-Frankfurt-Rome-Beirut-Bombay-Calcutta.

Another three 707s were delivered by April 1962 and all nine Super Constellations were transferred to the Indian Air Force. BOAC replaced the Comets on the London to Hong Kong route with 707s on 25th March 1962 and operated a weekly Comet service from Kuwait-Bahrain-Karachi-Bombay in 1962/63 for Air India. They also introduced VC10s on the London to Tokyo route in September 1964. Air India continued to expand and by 1968 had acquired three new 707-337Bs and two 707-320C freighters, with their first B747-237B operating to London on 21st May 1971. In 1972/73, the pool agreement was suspended, however a new agreement was signed by BOAC/Air India on 1st July 1973.

DH.106 Comet 4 G-APDE (c/n 6406), with Air India titles, taken at Kuwait on 9th June 1962.

BORNEO AIRWAYS 1957~1965

De Havilland DH.89A Rapide VR-OAC (c/n 6812) taken at Paya Lebar, Singapore in 1957.

Borneo Airways Limited was formed in October 1957 by the Governments of the territories of North Borneo, Sarawak and Brunei holding 51% shares and BOAC Associated Companies with 49%. By 1958 the airline, based on Labuan Island North Borneo, linked the three territories and operated to seventeen airfields with three ex-Malayan Airways' Rapides and two Twin Pioneers, with a third added in 1960. The Rapides were then sold when two Douglas DC-3s were bought.

The airline signed a pool agreement with Malaysian Airlines (MAL) in 1963 for the Kuching-Labuan-Brunei-Jesselton route and, by 1964, Borneo Airways operated scheduled services to Bintulu, Brunei Town, Kota Kinabalu, Keningau, Kuching, Kudat, Labuan, Miri, Marudi, Ranau, Sandakan, Sepulot, Sibu, Simanggang and Tawau. International services also operated from Labuan, with Malayan Airways to Kuching-Singapore, Cathay Pacific to Hong Kong and Manila and Qantas to Hong Kong and Australia.

On the 1st April 1965 Borneo Airways merged with Malaysian Airways and BOAC's 89,960 shares (valued at £104,954) were exchanged for Malaysian Airways' shares.

Douglas C-47B 9M-ANE (c/n 26237/14792) also at Paya Lebar on 23rd February 1965.

BORNEO AIRWAYS 1957~1965

Scottish Aviation Twin Pioneer 1 VR-OAE (c/n 507) in flight in full Borneo Airways' livery before delivery.

Scottish Aviation Twin Pioneer 1 9M-ANO (c/n 532) at Kuching, Sarawak in 1964.

Douglas C-47B VR-HDA (c/n 32991/16243) sits idle at Kai Tak Airport in 1959.

1959~1972

Douglas DC-6B VR-HFK (c/n 45496) on a test flight before delivery to the airline on 22nd June 1958.

Roy Farrell and Sydney de Kantzow, both ex-air force pilots in the Chinese National Aviation Corporation, formed Cathay Pacific Airways Ltd. (CPA) in Hong Kong on the 24th September 1946. They flew charter flights using two DC-3s throughout south-east Asia and occasionally to Australia and England, and introduced scheduled services from Hong Hong to Singapore, Bangkok, Rangoon and Manila.

In 1947 five additional DC-3s were bought and three PBY-5A Catalina amphibians, followed in January 1948 by two Avro Ansons. CPA was taken over on 18th October 1948 by Butterfield & Swire Ltd, a major local trading company who acquired 45% shares, and Australian National Airlines with 35%. It was registered as Cathay Pacific Airways (1948) Ltd.

Lockheed L-188A Electra at Kai Tak Airport, Hong Kong in 1960.

1959~1972

DC-4 VR-HFF (c/n 10412) was bought from Canadian Pacific in August 1954 and flew with Cathay Pacific for over nine years. The aircraft sits at Kai Tak Airport on the 10th August 1962 awaiting the next load of passengers.

with nominal capital of HK$10 million, with Farrell and de Kantzow both retaining 10% of the shares.

On the 13th May 1949, the local British Hong Kong Government granted the lucrative southern routes to Cathay and the northern routes to the BOAC owned Hong Kong Airways. A Cathay DC-4 upgraded the Hong Kong-Bangkok-Singapore route on the 23rd September 1949 and over the next

five years several DC-3s were sold. Cathay bought their first pressurised aircraft, a Douglas DC-6, in December 1954 and in 1958 a new DC-6B was added. The following year, on 24th April 1959, the first of two new turboprop Lockheed Electras began services from Hong Kong-Manila-Bangkok-Singapore. Meanwhile in 1958/59, BOAC agreed that Cathay Pacific should manage Hong Kong Airways with effect from 1st February 1959 and in

At Sydney, Australia, Bristol Britannia 102 G-ANBO (c/n12916) carries Cathay stickers during a lease period from BOAC in January 1961.

1959~1972

Douglas DC-6B VR-HFK (c/n 45496) is prepared for flight at Kai Tak Airport on the 20th July 1961.

July absorbed the airline in exchange for 15% of Cathay shares.

A second Electra was operated from the 9th July extending turboprop services to Saigon, Taipei, Tokyo, Kuala Lumpur and to Sydney via Darwin. However, the Electras suffered vibration problems and in March 1960 the F.A.A. issued an A.D. which restricted the speed to 295mph/475kph until modifications were embodied to strengthen engine installations and replace wing skins with thicker material. When the Electras returned to Lockheed in the USA for modifications, Cathay wet-leased two BOAC Britannia 102s which operated 79 services from December 1960 to February 1961 when the Electras returned to service and operated at the normal cruise speed of 373mph/603kph.

The airline ordered another new type, a medium-range Convair 880-22M four-engine pure jet, which was advertised as the fastest jetliner in the Orient with a cruising speed of 555mph/893kph

Lockheed Electra VR-HFN (c/n 1002) also taken at Kai Tak Airport on the 20th July 1961.

1959~1972

Convair 880M-22-M22 VR-HGG (c/n 22-7-8-60) prepares to land at Kai Tak in October 1972.

configured for 104 first/economy passengers. This went into service on the 8th April 1962 and, over the next eight years, Cathay purchased a further eight Convair 880s. The airline also acquired twelve Intercontinental Boeing 707-351s from Northwest Orient Airlines of the USA over three years for long-range routes, with the first service operated on the 24th August 1971. The Convairs served the company well and were in service until September 1975 when two Lockheed Tristars joined the fleet to operate short and medium

routes. On the 31st March 1974, BOAC still retained their trade investment of 15% of Cathay, 85,000 shares of HK$100 each, valued at £414,000.

On the 1st July 1948 Cathay Pacific formed a subsidiary, Macao Air Transport Co. Ltd. (MASCO), which leased their Catalinas for a twice daily scheduled service from Hong Kong to the Portuguese Colony of Macau on the coast of China only 40 miles/64 kms away where there was a legal

Boeing 707-351VR-HGH (c/n 18584) taxies in at Kai Tak Airport on the 20th April 1972.

1959~1963

Canadian Vickers-built OA-10A Catalina VR-HDH (c/n CV592/44-34081) taken at Kai Tak Airport.

casino. The amphibious Catalinas were configured for 23 passengers and operated from the Macau waterfront to Kai Tak Airport. On the 16th July 1948, one of the world's first attempted hijacking occurred when Catalina VR-HDT 'Miss Macao' returned from Macau to Hong Kong with a full load including four Chinese millionaires. Immediately after take-off, three armed passengers (Chinese pirates) attempted to take control of the aircraft.

Unfortunately Captain Dale Cramer and First Officer Ken McDuff were shot and the aircraft crashed with only one of the passengers surviving.

Catalina VR-HDS was sold in August 1950 but VR-HDH flew scheduled and charter services until 1960/61 when VR-HFP, a small Piaggio P-136-L2 amphibian, was bought which remained in service until at least 1963.

Piaggio P-136-L2 (c/n 243), a five-seat amphibian, powered by two 340hp Lycoming GSO-480-B1-C6 piston engines driving pusher-propellers, at Kai Tak on 10th August 1962.

1947~1959

Left:
Douglas C-47A Dakota 3 VR-HDN (c/n 12019) 'Kwang Tung' was G-AGJY. one of four-BOAC DC-3s chartered to HKA, which were overhauled at the BOAC Whitchurch base before closure in November 1948.

Hong Kong Airways Limited (HKA), registered on 4th March 1947, was a wholly-owned subsidiary of BOAC with capital of HK$396,000. The airline's four Dakotas and four crews came from BOAC whilst four stewardesses were selected from over 200 local Chinese applicants who spoke a minimum of three languages, were experienced in nursing and were very attractive! The C-47s were painted in Bristol with an attractive colour scheme with winged red lion logos, and a blue and silver cheat line with Chinese characters on the starboard side. Their first scheduled service, thrice weekly from Hong Kong to Shanghai, started on 2nd December 1947 followed on the 10th January with a twice daily service from Hong Kong to Guangzhou. This 40 minute flight was very popular and by the 22nd March services had increased to four per day.

A service was also opened from Hong Kong to Manila but the civil war in China reduced the airline's income and so BOAC sold the airline to Jardine Matheson and Co. Ltd. on 1st December 1949. Services to China eventually ceased and the DC-3s were sold, however HKA continued the Hong Kong-Taipei service with DC-3s charted from Cathay Pacific Airways (CPA).

In January 1956, BOAC Associated Companies Ltd. once again bought shares in Hong Kong Airways (50%) and leased two Viscounts to them to operate services to Seoul from 25th February 1957, to Manila in March, Taipei in April, and Tokyo in May. By December 1958 BOAC had acquired 100% shareholding, however there followed heavy losses and BOAC agreed to merge HKA with CPA. On the 1st February 1959, CPA took over the management of Hong Kong Airways and the two airlines merged on the 8th June, with BOAC receiving 15% shares in CPA.

Hong Kong Airways operated two long-range Vickers-Armstrong V.760D Viscounts. They were used initially from Hong Kong-Seoul, and later to Manila, Taipei and Tokyo. After the HKA/CPA merger, the two Viscounts went to Malayan Airways. Above we see VR-HFJ (c/n 187) at Kai Tak in 1957.

1947~1972

Airspeed AS.65 Consul VR-SCD (c/n 4324) was Malayan Airways' first aircraft, photo circa 1947.

Right:
De Havilland
DH.89A Rapide
VR-OAA (c/n 6908)
was operated by
Malayan Airways
in Borneo, and later
sold to Borneo
Airways in 1957,
photo circa 1955.

Douglas C-47A Dakota VR-SCO (c/n 13366) was registered in August 1947 to Malayan Airways.
Here we see 'Osprey' in the exotic location of Paya Lebar, Singapore on 16th September 1958.

1947~1972

Douglas C-54A-1-DO VR-SEA (c/n 7458) 'Albatross' at Paya Lebar on 17th October 1958.

Registered in Singapore on the 21st October 1937, Malayan Airways Ltd. was founded by Imperial Airways, the Straits Steamship Co. Ltd. of Singapore and the Ocean Steamship Co. Ltd of Liverpool. However Malayan Airways did not commence operations until 2nd April 1947 when a charter flight operated from Kallang Airport, Singapore to Simpang Airport, Kuala Lumpur with VR-SCD, an Airspeed Consul initially named 'Raja Udang' (Malay for Kingfisher). These small twin-engine aircraft carried five passengers and scheduled services began on 1st May 1947 from Singapore-Kuala Lumpur-Ipoh-Penang thrice weekly, taking 1hr 30mins to fly from Singapore to Kuala Lumpur and another two hours to Penang.

In the latter half of 1947, Malayan Airways signed an agreement with BOAC to provide advice, technical staff and aircraft. BOAC acquired 25,000 shares at M$10 each (10% shareholding) and arranged for five Dakotas, each fitted with 21 seats, to be delivered from August 1947 to expand the Malayan domestic routes and to begin international services from Singapore to Indonesia, Saigon, and later to Sarawak and North Borneo. In April 1948 a new service was inaugurated from Singapore to Bangkok followed, on 1st September 1949, with a service from Singapore to Mergui (in southern Burma) and Rangoon which operated for three years. In 1952 the airline phased out the Airspeed Consuls whilst the DC-3 fleet was increased to nine, and the service from Singapore to Kuala Lumpur increased to thrice daily. Three ex-BEAC DH.89A Dragon Rapides were delivered between 1952-1955 for domestic services in North Borneo, and later Brunei and Sarawak. When the new airport at Paya Lebar was opened on the 20th August 1955, Kallang Airport was closed.

Viscount V.760D 9M-ALY (c/n 186) seen at Paya Lebar on 7th October 1959.

1947~1972

On the 1st April 1958, Malayan Airways Ltd. was restructured with share capital increased to S$20 million with BOAC and Qantas each having 33% share-holding. A major expansion took place and Federation Air Services, which flew feeder services on the Malay peninsula into the hub airports of Kuantan, Kuala Lumpur, Kota Bharu and Ipoh with de Havilland DHC-2 Beavers, was also absorbed. A single Qantas Douglas C-54 Skymaster was leased to operate from Singapore to Hong Kong and on 1st August 1959 two long-range turboprop Viscounts leased from BOAC-AC replaced Dakotas on routes to Kuala Lumpur, North Borneo and Djakarta. Flight times were cut

Above: *Fokker F-27 Friendship Series 200 9M-AMM (c/n 10232) taken at Kuching in Sarawak, Borneo.*

Below: *Scottish Aviation Twin Pioneer 9M-ANC (c/n 519) was operated in Borneo.*

Bottom: *Twin Pioneer 9M-ANC (c/n 519) seen in the later livery.*

1947~1972

BOAC Comet 4 G-APDC (c/n 6404) is serviced at Kai Tak in April 1964, whilst under lease to Malaysian Airways.

and passenger comfort improved with reduced vibration and noise. The unpressurised Skymaster service was in competition with the pressurised DC-6s of Cathay Pacific Airways on the Singapore-Hong Kong route, but they became outclassed when Cathay replaced the DC-6s with two new turboprop Lockheed Electras and the Skymaster was replaced in April 1960 with two wet-leased Qantas Lockheed L-1049E Super Constellations, VH-EAG (c/n 4539) and VH-EAK (c/n 4573), for six months. When the two Electras needed modifications, they were flown to Lockheed in California and CPA leased a Bristol Britannia 102 from BOAC. Malayan and CPA then agreed to pool the Singapore-Hong Kong route with Malayan leasing a BOAC Britannia 102 in 1961.

In 1962, Malayan Airways leased BOAC Britannia 102s for a short time on routes to Hong Kong and Djakarta, but these were replaced in December with leased BOAC Comet 4s as they

became available. These were Malayan Airways' first pure jets and introduced the 'Silver Kris Jet' service from Singapore-Kuala Lumpur-Bangkok, Singapore-Kuching, Singapore-Jesselton (renamed Kota Kinabalu) and Singapore-Hong Kong. Soon after, in January 1963, a tripartite pool agreement was signed with THAI International and Cathay Pacific Airways on the Singapore-Kuala Lumpur-Bangkok and Hong Kong routes which were flown by Malayan Comets, THAI Convair 990s and Caravelle jets, whilst Cathay used Electras and Convair 880s. Five new Dutch-made Fokker F-27-200s were also delivered between March and May 1963 to replace the leased BOAC-AC Viscounts and to expand regional services throughout Malaysia and Borneo.

On the 16th September 1963 the Federation of Malaysia was formed by Malaya, Singapore and North Borneo (Sabah), with Sarawak (now known

Britannia 102 G-APLL (c/n 12908) at Kai Tak Airport on the 6th August 1962.

1947~1972

DH.106 Comet 4 9V-BAU (c/n 6406) taxies at Paya Lebar in the full colours of the airline after purchase from BOAC.

as East Malaysia) and Brunei staying independent. The airline was renamed Malaysian Airways to reflect the change, however, there was an anomaly in that Borneo Airways operated local services on the island of Borneo. A joint committee representing the Governments of the Malaysian Federation, Brunei and BOAC-AC decided, as of 1st April 1965, that Malaysian Airways would absorb Borneo Airways. With the utilisation of the leased Comets and the popularity of the 'Silver Kris Jet' service, Malaysian Airways decided to buy five Comet 4s from BOAC, with the first being delivered in September 1965.

On the 9th August 1965, under Prime Minister Lee Kwan Yew, a Straits-born Chinese who studied law at Cambridge University, the Singapore Government withdrew the country from the 'Federation' and Singapore became an Independent state. The following year, the Governments of

Malaysia and Singapore decided, on 14th May 1966, to acquire control of the airline and increased their share capital to S$100 million, with each Government holding 29.5% shareholding. They agreed on a name change to Malaysia-Singapore Airlines Ltd. (MSA) from 1st January 1967 and the airline became the national airline of both countries. BOAC still had 347,000 shares but this was now only 11.57% of the total shareholding.

On the 15th March 1967 the Malaysian Prime Minister, Tun Abdul Razak, announced that three Boeing 707-312Bs and five Boeing 737-112s had been ordered for delivery in 1968/1969, with the flying winged tiger symbol replaced with a stylised winged tiger. The 'Silver Kris Jet' Comet service was expanded from Singapore-Djakarta-Perth, and Singapore-Hong Kong-Taipei, and a new service began from Singapore to Manila. By the end of 1967, the airline had carried over one million passengers in

Douglas C-47B 9M-ANE (c/n 26237/14792) taken at Paya Lebar on 21st September 1970.

1947~1972

Fokker F-27-200 Friendship (c/n 10231) was originally delivered to Malayan Airways and registered 9M-AML in May 1963. When the airline was renamed Malaysia-Singapore Airlines on the 1st January 1967, the aircraft was re-registered as 9V-BAQ.

the previous twelve months. Expansion continued and in the following year a new route was opened from Singapore-Djakarta-Sydney operated by wet-leased Qantas Boeing 707s.

MSA's first new Boeing 707 arrived in June 1968 with a new black, white and yellow livery and the large new MSA logo covering the whole tail. New uniforms were introduced and the female flight attendants were dressed in striking sarong kebayas designed by the famous French couturiere Pierre Balmain. MSA joined a pool partnership with Air India, Air New Zealand, BOAC and Qantas for operations between South East Asia and Australia and, with the arrival of more Boeing 707s, the Singapore-Sydney service was increased to thrice weekly and the Singapore-Hong Kong-

Taipei route extended to Tokyo. Three small piston-engine Britten-Norman Islanders were bought in December 1968 for local services in East Malaysia and the following year, on 21st August 1969, the first of five Boeing 737-112s operated from Singapore-Kuala Lumpur-Penang-Bangkok and Singapore-Kuching, replacing the Comets which were phased out and sold to Dan Air of London.

In 1970 additional routes were added with 737s flying to Bali and 707s to Colombo and Madras. The Malaysian Government wanted to develop the country's vast resources and improve transportation and communications, and so eleven more Fokker F-27s and two Boeing 737s were ordered. However Singapore wanted to develop international routes via the Middle East

Ex-BOAC de Havilland Comet 4 9V-BAU (c/n 6406) at Heathrow in March 1968 after re-painting into MSA colours.

1947~1972

Boeing 707-312 9V-BBB (c/n 19739) seen in the new MSA livery at Paya Lebar in 1969.

and Europe and so it was decided to split MSA into two airlines. Malaysian Airline System (MAS) was incorporated in Kuala Lumpur on the 3rd April 1971 with Qantas supplying management and technical staff. MSA was still operating and inaugurated its first European service from Singapore-Bombay-Bahrain-Rome-London with a Boeing 707 on the 2nd June 1971.

On the 29th January 1972, Mercury-Singapore Airlines was registered in Singapore, but the name was changed to Singapore International Airlines Ltd. (SIA) on the 26th July 1972. Singapore had gained tremendous confidence since independence and the country was booming, so they ordered two Boeing 747-212Bs with two more on option. MSA was split on the 30th June 1972 and MAS was allocated S$200 million, nine Fokker F-27s and three Britten-Norman BN-2A Islanders. SIA was allocated five Boeing 707s, five Boeing 737s, two Fokker F-27s and retained the international routes from Singapore, the major business centre and cross-roads of South East Asia. When MSA ceased trading on 1st October 1972, BOAC had 4% shares.

The two new airlines began to operate services under their own names. MAS was based at Subang International Airport, Kuala Lumpur and their logo was a red Kelantan kite painted on the tails of their aircraft, whilst SIA was based at Paya Lebar and their logo, a yellow stylised bird, was proudly displayed on their aircraft.

Boeing 737-112 9V-BBC (c/n 19769) also at Paya Lebar on 31st August 1969.

1947~1972

At Heathrow on 10th May 1972, BOAC Boeing 707-436 G-APFI (c/n 17710) wears Malaysian Airline System stickers whilst under lease from BOAC to the airline.

707-324C 9V-BEY (c/n 19353) taxies at Osaka on 3th June 1974.

On lease from BA, 707-436 G-APFJ (c/n 17711) displays MAS's new colours on 5th December 1974.

ORIENT AIRWAYS
1946~1953

Convair CV-240-7 N90836 (c/n 240-82) (later AP-AEG) 'Orient Skyliner' in 1949.

Orient Airways was incorporated in Calcutta on the 23rd October 1946 by Merza Ahmed and Merza Abo Hassan Ispahani, under an initiative by Quaid-i-Azam Mohammad Ali Jinnah (founder of Pakistan). They began charter flights with Douglas DC-3s and the following year, on 30th June, a scheduled service was operated from Calcutta-Chittagong-Aykab-Rangoon, Burma.

Pakistan was founded on the 14th August 1947 and Orient Airways was given the responsibility to link East and West Pakistan with BOAC seconding technical and commercial staff to the airline. On the 1st October three weekly services were inaugurated with DC-3s from Dacca (East Pakistan) via Calcutta and Delhi in India to Karachi (West Pakistan), a 13hr trip, as well as services from Dacca-Calcutta and Dacca-Chittagong. The following day, domestic services were opened within West Pakistan from Karachi-Lahore-Rawalpindi-Peshawa, and Karachi-Quetta-Lahore.

Orient Airways moved its headquarters and main base to Karachi on 2nd January 1948. The airline had a fleet of 20+ Douglas DC-3s, two Beech 18s and two Stinsons, and they also ordered three Convair 240s to fly direct from West to East Pakistan (1,100 miles/1,770 kms). A military service also began on the 12th February 1949 when DC-3s flew into Kashmir from Peshawar-Gilgit-Skardu, and the service from Karachi-Delhi-Calcutta-Dacca was inaugurated on 1st May 1949.

Four years later, on 1st October 1953, Orient Airways was merged with the state-owned Pakistan International Airlines (PIA) but continued to operate as Orient until 11th March 1955 when it was fully integrated. In May 1964, BOAC signed a partnership agreement with PIA for the Karachi-London route and PIA services via Moscow but the agreement was terminated six years later on 30th September 1970.

Convair CV-240-7 AP-AEF (c/n 240-75) seen wearing the newly acquired livery of PIA 1955.

1946~1954

Leased ANA DC-4 VH-ANB (c/n 42948) 'Lackrana' at Essendon Airport, Melbourne in 1947.

On the 24th June 1946, British Commonwealth Pacific Airlines Ltd. (BCPA) was registered in Sydney with £1million capital by the Governments of Australia (50%), UK (20%) and New Zealand (30%). The nominees were Qantas (50%), BOAC (20%) and TEAL (30%).

Four DC-4s were initially leased from Australian National Airways (ANA) for the 'Southern Cross' trans-Pacific route from Sydney-Fiji-Canton Island-Honolulu-San Francisco (7,591 miles/12,216 kms) which took 44 flying hours spread over three days. This service operated twice monthly from the 15th September 1946 and was later extended from San Francisco to Vancouver. On 25th April 1947 a monthly service operated from Auckland-Fiji-Canton Island-Honolulu-San Francisco-Vancouver.

The ANA aircraft were replaced with BCPA's own DC-4s, but these were also replaced in December 1948

when BCPA took delivery of four new DC-6s which were configured with 37 sleeper berths. These were named after the sailing vessels of Captain James Cook - Adventure, Discovery, Endeavour and Resolution.

BCPA built up an excellent reputation for its professionalism, punctuality and personal service. The airline was profitable and in February 1952 ordered six 44-seat Comet 2s for delivery in 1954, but this was later reduced to three. A meeting of the South Pacific Air Transport Council (SPATC) took place in October 1953 in Christchurch where it was decided that Qantas would take over BCPA and operate the trans-Pacific route with their new Lockheed Super Constellations. The three remaining DC-6s were transferred to TEAL who would operate the New Zealand-Australia and New Zealand-Fiji services. The merger took effect on 15th May 1954 and BOAC ceased to have holdings in BCPA and TEAL.

Douglas DC-6 VH-BPG (c/n 43127) 'Adventure' is shot while on delivery at San Francisco in November 1948. Note the upper berth windows and airline's route map marked on the fin.

AIR MELANESIÆ 1960~1972

Australian-built de Havilland Australia DHA 3 Drover 3b VP-PAP (c/n 5011) 'Big Narbas' seen at Bankstown Sydney in June 1970. when flying for Air Melanesia, a subsidiary of Fiji Airways.

Fiji Airways was founded by Harold Gatty in July 1951 at Suva, the capital of Viti Levu, Fiji. It was Gatty who had navigated the Lockheed Vega 'Winnie Mae' round the world flight in 1931 from Rhoosevelt Field, New York-Gander-UK-Germany-Russia-Alaska-Canada and back to New York flown by one-eyed pilot Wiley Post in eight days, 15hrs and 51mins.

On the 1st September 1951, using a de Havilland DH.89 Rapide, services were inaugurated from Nausori Airport, Suva on the east coast to Nadi, Fiji's international airport on the west coast of Viti Levu, and in December to Lambasa on the island of Vanua Levu. Another Rapide was added in February 1952 and later, in October 1953, a service began to the smaller island of Taveuni. It is believed that in July 1954 Qantas acquired 50% shares of Fiji Airways and an unconfirmed report of BOAC having 5% shares. Qantas supplied Fiji Airways with two of their de Havilland Australia DHA 3 Drovers.

Following the death of Harold Gatty on the 10th August 1957, Qantas acquired the remain-

De Havilland Heron 1B VQ-FAY (c/n 14011) at Nausori Suva, Fiji in November 1966.

FIJI AIRWAYS 1960~1972

Douglas C-47A VH-EDC (c/n 12874) taken at Brisbane on the 26th June 1966, in the company of a BOAC Boeing 707.

ing shares and took control of Fiji Airways on the 24th March 1958. In 1959, two de Havilland Heron 1Bs, ex-NZNAC, were bought via Qantas to expand services to Tonga and 50% of the shares were sold to TEAL. On the 1st January 1960, Fiji Airways was re-financed and split between Qantas, who retained management control, TEAL and BOAC-AC with each holding 33% of issued share capital of £157,000. An ex-Qantas single-engine de Havilland Canada DHC-2 Beaver with amphibious floats was bought for services from Suva-Levuka and Suva-Kapavu starting on 4th March 1960 as well as for charter

flights from Suva's beach.

In 1961 the fleet consisted of three British Herons, three Australian Drovers and a single Canadian Beaver, a very unusual combination of de Havilland aircraft from three continents. In 1962 the airline also acquired Korolevu Air Transport with their single Piper Caribbean. The Heron 2s, with a crew of Captain, First Officer/Navigator and Engineer/Steward operated long-range routes from Fiji to Funafuti in the Ellice Islands (564 miles) and on to Tarawa

HS.748 Series 2A VQ-FBH (c/n 1661) at Woodford on 27th November 1968.

AIR PACIFIC 1960~1972

Britten-Norman BN-2A-III Trislander G-BCJX (c/n 0391) taken in flight between the islands in 1973.

in the Gilberts (700 miles). In 1966 the Heron fleet was increased to seven and the following year a DC-3 was chartered from Qantas. The first of three HS.748s was delivered whilst the Drovers were phased out. Services were expanded and routes inaugurated to Apia in Western Samoa, Port Vila in New Hebrides, Honiara in the British Solomon Islands, and Nauru Island and Port Moresby in Papua New Guinea. The HS.748s also operated services for Air New Zealand from Nadi to Raratonga in the Cook Islands between September 1970 and December 1972.

In 1970 co-operation agreements were signed with Polynesian Airlines of Samoa and Air New Zealand and, from the 31st July 1971, Fiji Airways changed its name to Air Pacific Ltd. and introduced new colours and logo. The first BAC 1-11 was delivered in March 1972 and operated as far afield as Auckland, Brisbane, Pago Pago in American Samoa, and Papeete in Tahiti.

BOAC's shares in Air Pacific were transferred to British Airways on its formation on 1st April 1974.

HS.748 Series 2A DQ-FBH (c/n 1661), taxies at Nausori Suva, Fiji in May 1972

FIJI AIRWAYS 1960~1972

Air Pacific DH Heron DQ-FAF (c/n 14123) sports the new colours of Air Pacific in March 1973.

BAC 1-11-479FU DQ-FBV (c/n 250) at Eagle Farm, Brisbane, November 1973.

De Havilland DH.86A VH-USC (c/n 2307) 'Canberra' flies over Australia in 1934.

1940~1974

Consolidated 32-3 Liberator II G-AGKU (c/n 45) at Sydney in August 1947.

On the 18th January 1934, Qantas Empire Airways Ltd. (QEA), known as Qantas, was registered to combine the interests of Queensland and Northern Territory Aerial Services Ltd. (Q.A.N.T.A.S.) and that of Imperial Airways Ltd (IAL) to operate an extension of the 'Empire Route' from London to Singapore and onwards to Brisbane, Australia. The two companies each held 49% of the shares with 2% held by an independent 'umpire' to resolve any disagreements in the partnership and the first Managing Director was Hudson Fysh from Q.A.N.T.A.S.

In April 1934, Qantas (QEA) was awarded government contracts for the carriage of mail from Brisbane-Darwin and Darwin-Singapore. Scheduled flights started on the 9th December 1934 with Darwin-Singapore initially operated by Imperial Airways' Atalantas until Qantas took over on the 25th February 1935 from Brisbane-Darwin-Singapore, a distance of 4,360 miles/7017 kms which took three and a half days with their new DH.86As. Qantas had previously asked de Havilland to modify their DH.86 design with dual controls for a Captain/Navigator and a First Officer/Radio Officer, and fitted with long-range fuel tanks for the Timor Sea crossing from Darwin-Koepang. The DH.86A's cabin was fitted for ten passengers and had a good cruising speed of 143mph/230kph.

Avro Lancastrian VH-EAV (c/n 1281), carrying a spare Constellation engine, prepares to depart Sydney in 1948.

1940~1974

Consolidated 28 Catalina G-AGFM/FP244 (c/n 145) Qantas No. 2 'Altair Star' at Lake Koggala on 10th July 1943.

In 1938 Qantas moved to Rose Bay, Sydney and took delivery of six Short S.23 'C' Class Empire flying boats fitted with the Sperry A2 automatic pilot for a Sydney to London service which opened on the 5th July 1938. They carried seventeen passengers in luxury, and in-flight catering consisted of sumptuous three course dinners that had been cooked on the ground and kept warm in vacuum flasks. The flight time from Australia to England was reduced to nine and half days, and this route was operated successfully for three and half years until 8th December 1941 when the Japanese bombed Singapore, thus the Empire service was terminated.

Hudson Fysh opened the Perth to Koggala Lake Ceylon (now Sri Lanka) ser-

Above: Catalina G-AGFM 'Altair Star' Qantas No. 2, and behind G-AGIE (c/n 183) 'Antares Star' Qantas No. 4, at Nedlands, Swan River, Perth.

Below: Lockheed 14-H Super Electra VH-ADT (c/n 1409) carried as many as fourteen passengers on vital domestic wartime routes. In 1944 it flew Melbourne - Townville, and the following year a weekly Brisbane-Darwin service. It was withdrawn in 1947.

1940~1974

Avro Lancastrian VH-EAS surveyed a route between Australia-South Africa in 1948.

Left:
A close up of Avro 691 Lancastrian VH-EAS (c/n 1184) with the crew who performed a survey flight across the Indian Ocean during November 1948. The aircraft flew Sydney-Perth-Cocos Islands-Mauritius-Johannesburg, in a flight time of 40hrs 14mins spread over six days.

Taken on the 27th November 1948 on arrival at Johannesburg, the crew (standing left to right) are:
Engineer Officer G H Hebron,
First Officer G Jakimov,
Captain in Command L R Ambrose,
Capt A R H Morris,
Senior Navigation Officer J L B Cowan and
Radio Officer W R Clarkson.

Lancastrian VH-EAT (c/n 1191) ex-BOAC G-AGML 'Nicobar' at Cocos Islands circa 1947.

1940~1974

vice with five Catalinas obtained from the RAF via BOAC, and flights began in July 1943 in total secrecy and in radio silence across the Indian Ocean. These aircraft were designed for an 'all-up weight' (AUW) of 27,000lbs, but for this operation 35,000lbs was not uncommon. At take-off the aircraft carried seven tons of fuel, with mail and priority passengers, and an overload of up to four tons required special techniques. On take-off, the control column was held central as full power was applied, then when effective control was gained, the pilot

pulled the controls hard back to bring the nose up and put the Catalina 'on the step'. The crew had limited weather information and no long-range radio navigation, and so relied on celestial navigation and dead reckoning. Liberator LB-30s which arrived on 17th June 1944 supplemented the Catalinas which stayed on until the 18th July 1945 after 271 services.

Meanwhile a new joint BOAC/Qantas service was inaugurated on the 31st May 1945 with Lancastrians from Hurn-Lydda-Karachi-Ceylon-

Short S.23 VH-ABA (c/n S.876) at Rose Bay in 1941. This image is one of the first colour photographs taken in Australia.

1940~1974

Lockheed 749A Constellation VH-EAB (c/n 2565) 'Lawrence Hargrave' in flight during 1947.

Learmouth-Sydney, with the return from Sydney to the UK on the 2nd June. Three Qantas pilots who developed the Indian Ocean route, Captains L.R. Ambrose, W.H. Crother and R.B. Tapp, were awarded the Johnson Memorial Trophy by the Guild of Air Pilots and Navigators for their outstanding navigation. When peace returned to the area, Qantas was already looking ahead and took a wise decision to order four Lockheed L-749 Constellations for use on the 'Kangaroo' route from Sydney to London.

On the 21st March 1947, the Australian Commonwealth Government bought 49% of BOAC's shareholding in Qantas, followed by the Q.A.N.T.A.S. shareholding in Qantas on 30th June. Now Government owned, it became the Australian flag carrier and the close working relationship between Qantas and BOAC continued, not only on the Kangaroo route but in other ventures with airlines of common interest in south-east Asia and the Pacific. Soon after this, Qantas surveyed new routes to New Guinea,

A Qantas Empire Airways DC-3 is caught loading snacks, fresh fruit, ice and a large thermos flask on-board at Archerfield Airport, Brisbane, Australia, during 1947.

1940~1974

Short Sandringham VH-EBX (c/n SH.32C) 'Pacific Chieftain', rides the swell at Rose Bay, Sydney in May 1950.

Norfolk Island and Lord Howe Island and, on 5th December 1947, a Qantas Lockheed L-749 Constellation completed the first flight from Sydney to London. This service was operated by VH-EAD 'Charles Kingsford Smith' and flown by Captain K.G. Jackson to Karachi and Captain D.F. McMasters to London. Qantas now operated the longest air route in the world.

In 1950 Douglas DC-4s came into service from Sydney-Port Moresby, New Guinea then, on 1st September 1952, the 'Wallaby' route was opened by VH-EAD 'Charles Kingsford

Smith' from Sydney to South Africa via Melbourne-Perth-Cocos-Mauritius and Johannesburg. In September 1953 Qantas operated DC-4s from Sydney-Brisbane-Port Moresby-Lae and expanded local services within New Guinea with DC-3s. On the 15th May 1954, the tripartite British Commonwealth Pacific Airlines (BCPA) was liquidated as the British Government decided to withdraw from participation. The three Douglas DC-6s went to Tasman Empire Airlines Ltd. (TEAL) and the trans-Pacific route went to Qantas. It was not long after the arrival of the Lockheed L-1049

Lockheed 1049G Super Constellation VH-EAO (c/n 4679) 'Southern Aurora' sits idle at Kai Tak, Hong Kong on 3rd December 1957.

1940~1974

L-1049G Super Constellation VH-EAF (c/n 4579) and DC-4 VH-EBK (c/n 42917) await passengers at Port Moresby in November 1959.

Super Constellation when services started, on 15th May 1954, from Sydney to San Francisco and to Vancouver which Qantas named the Southern Cross route. Qantas built up a fleet of sixteen Super Constellations and by January 1958 operated a round-the-world service in two directions, via the USA and the Middle East, carrying up to 82 passengers and cruising at 335mph/539kph.

These Qantas aircraft developed global services over the next four years, and by January 1958 you could fly around the world in five and a half days eastbound or six days westbound. On 24th March 1958 Qantas bought controlling shares in Fiji Airways and the following year, after considering the purchase of Bristol Britannias, ordered seven long-range Boeing 707-138s for intercontinental services. This was a large jet aircraft in comparison with the L-1049 and carried more passengers at higher speeds of 550mph/885kph, thus reducing flight times by almost a half. The early Pratt and Whitney JT3C pure jets were later replaced with

Taken at Port Moresby in November 1959, de Havilland Canada DHC-3 Otter VH-EAW (c/n 240) 'Kikori', fitted with Edo amphibious floats and a 600hp Pratt and Whitney Wasp engine, was operated by Qantas in Papua New Guinea.

1940~1974

Douglas C-47A VH-EAR (c/n 12035) taken at Papua New Guinea in November 1959.

JT3D turbofans which gave greater economy and range. Qantas was the first airline to provide a round-the-world jet service via New York, and the airline also took delivery of Lockheed Electras which replaced the Super Constellations on Australasia routes including a service operated in parallel with TEAL to New Zealand.

On the 1st August 1967, the airline changed its name to Qantas Airways Ltd. and there would be a lengthy period before Qantas received its next new type, the Boeing 747, the first of which was intro-duced into service in September 1971 and carried up to 433 passengers depending on the Series.

The airline has had in service a comprehensive range of 747s, including 747Bs, Series 200s, 300s, 400s and the 747SP. These aircraft operated the main trunk routes and replaced the faithful Boeing 707. The airline has come a long way since Q.A.N.T.A.S. was formed on the 16th November 1920 and it has the distinction of being the second oldest airline in the world, with a safety record that is second to none.

DHC-3 Otter VH-EAZ (c/n 258) 'Kerowagi' at Wau, Papua New Guinea in 1959.

1940~1974

Lockheed 1049C Super Constellation VH-EAG (c/n 4539) 'Southern Constellation' taken in flight, April 1954.

Lockheed 1049H Super Constellation VH-EAM (c/n 4801) 'Southern Spray', while under charter to BOAC, starts its engines at Heathrow in May 1962.

Douglas C-47A VH-EDC (c/n 12874) taken at Sydney on 12th September 1961.

1940~1974

Boeing 707-138 VH-EBE (c/n 17700) 'City of Perth' on a test flight in August 1959.

A very rare shot of BOAC Comet 4 G-APDL (c/n 6413) taken at Heathrow in March 1960, wearing Qantas stickers while on charter to the airline.

Boeing 707-338C VH-EAD (c/n 19624) 'City of Melbourne' at Sydney in April 1968.

1940~1974

Short S.30 'C' Class ZK-AMC (c/n S.886) 'Awarua' (Two Rivers) taken at Rose Bay, Sydney in 1940.

Tasman Empire Airways Ltd. was founded in April 1940 by the Governments of New Zealand, Australia and the UK, represented by Union Airways of New Zealand with 39%, BOAC with 38% and QEA with 23% shareholdings. Three Short S.30 flying-boats configured for fifteen passengers were transferred from BOAC to TEAL to extend the UK to Sydney route through to Auckland. However the second S.30, ZK-AMB (c/n S.885) 'Australia', was seriously damaged on its delivery flight whilst landing at Basra, and after a lengthy rebuild was returned to BOAC under its original registration G-AFCZ and named 'Clare'. The

two TEAL Empire flying-boats 'Awarua' and 'Ao-tea-roa' inaugurated the trans-Tasman service initially from Waitemata Harbour, Auckland (later Mechanics Bay) to Rose Bay, Sydney on the 30th April 1940 with a scheduled flight time of 10hrs.

Over the next five years, the Short S.30s carried 14,899 passengers, 601,089lbs of mail and 225,366lbs of freight in over 1,000 flights with no loss, a remarkable achievement. It is also reported that they were fitted with search radar and flew several military reconnaissance missions in WWII throughout the Pacific Islands and once operated

Short S.30 'C' Class ZK-AMA (c/n S.884) 'Ao-tearoa' (Long White Cloud) seen at Rochester on 6th April 1939.

1940~1974

Above:
Powered by four 2,040hp Bristol Hercules 773 engines, Short S.45 Solent Mk.4 ZK-AMM (c/n SH.1557) named 'Ararangi' (Way through the Skies) takes-off in 1949.

Left:
Solent ZK-AMM returns from a test flight prior to delivery to TEAL in 1949. The insignia on the bow is the 'Maroro', the Maori symbol for the flying fish.

Below:
Short S.45 Solent Mk.3 G-AKNR (c/n S.1296) 'City of Belfast', taken in Belfast before delivery via Gander-San Francisco-Honolulu-Fiji-Auckland. It was renamed 'Aparimu' (Grouping of Five) and registered ZK-AMQ.

1940~1974

Ex-BCPA Douglas DC-6 ZK-BGA (c/n 43126) 'Aotearoa III' at Sydney in February 1960.

as far afield as Honolulu. On the 17th July 1946 the first of four Short S.25 Sandringham 4 'Tasman class' flying boats (ZK-AMB) was delivered to operate the Tasman service, which continued until the 29th October 1947. However the aircraft suffered persistent problems with the 1,200hp Pratt and Whitney R-1830 Twin Wasp engines overheating and it was nearly two years before the first of four Short S.45 Solent 4s, ZK-AMM 'Ararangi', was delivered to replace

them, arriving on the 29th September 1949.

With these powerful Solents a new service from Wellington to Sydney was opened and the troublesome Sandringhams were replaced and sold. A single Catalina was acquired and used for surveying Pacific Island routes and, on the 27th December 1951, the 'Coral Route' was inaugurated once a month with the Solents from Auckland-Suva, Fiji-Aitutaki and the

Lockheed L-188C Electra ZK-CLX (c/n 2007) 'Akaroa' taken at Sydney on 26th November 1965.

1940~1974

Cook Islands-Papeete, Tahiti, increased to twice monthly on the 26th May.

British Commonwealth Pacific Airlines was merged into Qantas on the 15th May 1954 and TEAL received BCPA's three Douglas DC-6s in exchange for their 30% shareholding. The British Government gave up their TEAL shares in April/May 1954 so that TEAL was owned equally by the Australian and New Zealand Governments, operating in association with BOAC and later British Airways. TEAL now had its first landplanes and quickly had the pressurised DC-6s in service, from Auckland to Sydney and also on the 'Hibiscus Service' from Auckland to Nadi connecting with the Qantas trans-Pacific service to the USA. On 29th June a weekly service was also inaugurated from Christchurch to Melbourne. Sector times were reduced dramatically and the Solents were withdrawn except for ZK-AMO 'Aranui' (Maori for Main Pathway) which flew the Suva-Papeete route which the aircraft operated until 15th September

1940~1974

McDonnell Douglas DC-8-84F ZK-NZD (c/n 45932) served twenty-one years with the airline.

1960 when it returned to Auckland with honour and was eventually placed on display at MOTAT.

TEAL acquired a 50% share of Fiji Airways, now jointly owned with Qantas, and it was on the 15th November 1959 that the first of three turbo-prop Lockheed L-188C Electras arrived. They had been recommended by Qantas and would replace the DC-6s which were transferred to the RNZAF.

On the 1st April 1961 TEAL became wholly owned by the New Zealand Government when it acquired the Qantas shareholding. TEAL wanted to expand its horizons to the USA and Asia and so ordered three new Douglas DC-8s. The company was renamed Air New Zealand Ltd. (ANZ) on the 1st April 1965 and this appeared on the DC-8 which arrived on 20th July 1965. The DC-8s were quickly put into service and inaugurated the Auckland-Suva-Honolulu-San Francisco route on 10th December and later to Hong Kong and Singapore. In January 1973 the first of three MDC-10-30s went into service and, at the end of 1973, the ANZ MDC-10 service from Auckland-Honolulu-Los Angeles was extended to London as a BOAC service with BOAC crews.

McDonnell Douglas MDC-10-30 ZK-NZL (c/n 47846) at La Tontouta Airport, Noumea on the 14th July 1977.

1949~1967

Ex-BOAC Canadair C-4 G-ALHR (c/n 163) 'Antiope' wears Aden stickers at Heathrow during February 1960.

Aden Airways Limited was registered on the 7th March 1949 as a wholly-owned BOAC subsidiary, with authorized capital of £225,000. Operations began on the 1st October 1949, initially from Almaza (Cairo), Asmara (Eritrea) and Khormaksar (Aden) with six ex-BOAC DC-3s on a route network previously operated by BOAC's No.5 Line, based at Cairo, to countries bordering the Red Sea, to Arabia, and the Horn of Africa.

By February 1950 services operated from Aden-Djibouti-Addis Ababa, Aden-Asmara-Port Sudan-Jeddah-Cairo, Aden-Mukerais, and Aden-Riyan which was later extended to Bahrain. Services were also introduced to connect with BOAC trunk routes at Nairobi and Khartoum from Aden-Asmara-Khartoum and Aden-Hargeisha-

Below: Douglas C-47 VR-AAZ (c/n 4495), ex-OD-AAM of MEA, is serviced on the ramp at Khormaksar in June 1964.

Below: Aden Airways DH Rapide VR-AAL (c/n 6700) 'Dhala' sits idle at Khormaksar in November 1955.

1949~1967

Vickers Viscount V.760D VR-AAW (c/n 186) at Wymeswold, England in May 1967.

Mogadishu-Nairobi. Two Avro Anson Mk.1s from Gulf Aviation were added to the fleet in June and July 1952.

In February 1953, the BOAC London-Rome-Cairo service was extended to Aden, operated by Hermes 4s, and later by Canadair C-4 Argonauts until the service was suspended in November 1956 because of the Suez crisis. In 1956, six additional DC-3s and two DH.89A Rapides were bought to expand local services and as the Argonauts proved popular, three more were bought from BOAC in 1960. The first was delivered on the 18th February and operated ten days later from Aden-Riyan-Sharjah-Bahrain, followed in May when they operated from Aden-Jeddah-Cairo and Aden-Hargeisa-

Mogadishu-Nairobi. In 1962, the airline received the Cumberbatch Trophy because of its good safety record.

In 1964 the Argonauts were replaced by two ex-Malayan Airways' Viscount V.760Ds which operated to Bahrain, Cairo, Khartoum, Mombassa and Nairobi. Pooling agreements were also signed with Air India International, East African Airways, Ethiopian Airlines and Sudan Airways. Because of political unrest in Aden, however, and following an in-flight explosion on one of their DC-3s which was subsequently lost and also the sabotage of Viscount VR-AAV which was totally destroyed, Aden Airways ceased operations and was finally closed down on the 30th June 1967.

Viscount V.760D VR-AAV (c/n 187) is serviced at Khartoum in May 1964.

1953~1958

Avro 685 York C.1 JY-ABZ (c/n 1302) 'Petra' at Beirut in September 1956.

In June 1946, Arab Airlines Association Ltd. (AAA) was formed in Amman by British and Trans-Jordanian interests. Operations began in November 1946 with five de Havilland DH.89A Rapides on domestic routes, then later operating to Baghdad, Beirut, Cairo, Haifa and Jerusalem. The airline also operated three DH.82A Tiger Moths and several Percival Proctors for their flying club/school.

On 1st August 1953, BOAC bought 49% of the company, now renamed Arab Airways (Jerusalem) Ltd and introduced DC-3s on routes to Beirut, Cairo, Baghdad and Kuwait. The airline was administered as an associate company of Aden Airways, who chartered two DC-3s to Arab Airways for services from Amman-Jeddah-Aden and Jerusalem-Aqaba-Jeddah-Aden. In 1955 both airlines came under the umbrella of Associated British Airlines (Middle East) Ltd.

Two Avro Yorks were leased from Skyways to operate Hadj flights to Mecca; JY-ABZ in 1956 and JY-AAC in 1957. On 31st October 1958, however, the airline ceased operations. By this time, it had operated an unduplicated route network of 4,969 miles/7,997 kms, with a final year income of £200,243 but expenditure of £227,468. With this loss, BOAC relinquished its interest in Arab Airways, which was then merged with Air Jordan on the 1st December 1958 to form Air Jordan of the Holy Land.

Douglas C-47B JY-ABN (c/n 25806/14361) 'Jerusalem' is maintained at Beirut in 1956.

1951~1974

DH.106 Dove 1B G-AMZJ (c/n 04429) awaits passengers at Doha in July 1958.

The Gulf Aviation Co. Ltd. (GA) was formed on 14th February 1950 in Bahrain by Frederick Bosworth (an aircraft engineer and ex-RAF pilot) and Bahraini interests. Approval for operations was given by Shaikh Salman bin Hamad Al Khalifa, Ruler of Bahrain, while his advisor Charles Belgrave became GA's Chairman. The company was then incorporated in London on the 24th March 1950.

The fleet consisted of Fairchild Argus type 2/3s and Avro Anson Mk.1s, based at RAF Muharraq,

Bahrain. Scheduled services were inaugurated by Ansons from Bahrain to Doha and to Sharjah on the 5th July 1950, four times per week, and Bahrain to Dhahran on the 25th, three times daily. By 1951 the fleet had expanded with five Ansons and three DH.86B bi-planes, but modern aircraft were needed and Freddie Bosworth travelled to England in May to purchase Doves and to discuss GA's future operations with BOAC. He signed a five year agreement with BOAC on the 24th May and bought an ex-East African Airways' Dove, however, on the 9th June

DH.114 Heron 1B G-APKW (c/n 14046) at Bahrain in 1959.

1951~1974

Fokker F-27-200 (c/n 10316) carrying reg. no. G-AVDN, later re-registered as A40-FN.

from Kuwait to Bahrain, Doha, Sharjah and Dubai until December 1969 when GA introduced their first jet, the BAC 1-11. These aircraft later inaugurated services in December 1970 to Shiraz in Iran, and the following year to Karachi and Bombay.

Intercontinental services began on the 1st April operated by BOAC VC10s from London-Doha-Dubai, and on the 4th April from London-Bahrain-Abu Dubai. Also in April, Gulf Aviation formed Gulf Helicopters Ltd. at Doha, Qatar to support the local oil industry. Two sturdy Short Skyvans were acquired in late 1970 for charter operations, and these were

joined by two BN Islanders in 1972.

With the planned sale of GA on the 1st April 1974 and the sale of four BOAC VC10s to Gulf Air, the first two (G-ARVI and G-ARVL) were painted during March 1974 in Gulf Air's livery of aubergine, green and red cheat-lines on a white fuselage and tail, ready for their inaugural 'Golden Falcon' flight on the 1st April 1974 from Bahrain to Heathrow. All BOAC shares in Gulf Aviation were sold to Gulf Air, formed by the Foundation Treaty signed on 1st April 1974, by the Rulers of Bahrain, Oman, Qatar and the United Arab Emirates, all with equal shares.

Short SC.7 Skyvan 3 A40-SO (c/n SH.1886) at Bahrain in February 1977.

KUWAIT AIRWAYS اكظلوط الجوبة الكويتية 1953~1967

Above: *Handley Page HP.81 Hermes 4 G-ALDU (c/n HP81/21) was leased for six months in 1956 from British charter carrier Britavia Ltd of the UK.*

Above: *Canadair C-4 G-ALHU (c/n 166) was leased from parent carrier BOAC also for six months during 1956.*

Below: *Kuwait National Airways DC-3 G-AMVA (c/n 33163/16415) was maintained and operated by British International Air Lines when in use by the airline.*

اكطوط الجوية الكويتية
KUWAIT AIRWAYS 1953~1967

Comet 4 G-APDS (c/n 6419) of BOAC at Heathrow on 6th December 1965, wearing Kuwait stickers during a period of lease to the airline.

British International Air Lines (BIAL) was formed in 1953 as a BOAC wholly-owned subsidiary based in Kuwait. It had two DC-3s available for charters, which they leased to the Kuwait Oil Company Ltd. (KOC).

Late in 1953 the Ruler of Kuwait and private interests founded Kuwait National Airways Ltd. (KNA) which was officially formed in March 1954. KNA then signed a contract with BIAL for technical assistance, aircrew and maintenance for their DC-3s, and operations began on the 17th May 1954 from Kuwait to Basra, and later the same month from Kuwait-Jerusalem and Kuwait-Damascus-Beirut.

1955 proved to be a busy time for BIAL. In April, their two DC-3s were replaced with two Vikings, followed in June with the company becoming a subsidiary of ABAMEL. In October, their Viking G-AGRU had a mishap at Basra and, whilst under repair, an Eagle Aircraft Services Viking, G-AHPM, was leased. BIAL also received a contract from the Kuwait Government to maintain eight Auster trainers for the Kuwait Flying School.

Vickers Viscount V.702 G-APTA (c/n 71) photographed at Karachi during May 1960.

KUWAIT AIRWAYS 1953~1967

De Havilland Comet 4C 9K-ACE (c/n 6474) on a test flight prior to delivery to the airline in January 1964.

Also in 1955 KNA changed its name to Kuwait Airways Ltd. when the Kuwaiti Government acquired 50% holdings. With this cash injection, the airline leased two Britavia Ltd. Hermes for six months, G-ALDU and G-ALDX, and these commenced operations from Kuwait-Damascus-Cairo on 25th June 1956, from Kuwait-Beirut on the 26th, and from Kuwait-Bahrain on the 27th. During 1956, BOAC's Argonaut G-ALHU 'Artimus' was also leased for 6 months, followed in 1957/58 when a Westair Ltd. Curtiss C-46 was leased to operate on Hadj flights and Universal Airlines Douglas C-54s were leased for scheduled services. BIAL then increased its fleet with the addition of two Scottish Aviation Twin Pioneers in October 1957 and a Viscount, which replaced the Vikings, in October 1958, all operating for the Kuwait Oil Company.

Vickers Viscount 776D G-APNF (c/n 225) shot at Beirut on 9th January 1959 in KAL livery.
The aircraft was leased by the Kuwait Oil Company and used by the Sheikh of Kuwait.

KUWAIT AIRWAYS 1953~1967

الخطوط الجوية الكويتية

Trident 1E 9K-ACF (c/n 2114), shot on an early test flight in March 1966.

On the 23rd May 1958, BOAC-AC signed a five year agreement with Kuwait Airways, effective from 1st June 1958, to take over management and operation of the airline, and to provide technical staff and new aircraft. A leased MEA Viscount arrived on the 1st June, followed by another in July then four leased BOAC-AC Viscounts between 1958-1960. By 1st January 1959, all scheduled services were operated by Viscounts, with the last two DC-3s sold to Gulf Aviation. BIAL was then merged with Kuwait Airways on the 1st April 1959.

In May 1962 the Kuwaiti Government acquired control of Kuwait Airways which they renamed the Kuwait Airways Corporation (KAC) and in August ordered two Comet 4Cs and three Trident 1Es (with one on option). In April 1964, KAC bought Trans Arabia Airways and acquired three DC-6Bs which replaced some Viscount services, including the Kuwait-Bahrain service for Gulf Aviation. The first Comet 4C, delivered in January 1963, operated Middle East services and when joined by the second Comet in February 1964, KAC joined the BOAC/MEA pool for the London-Middle East-Persian Gulf route until September 1966. KAC also leased several BOAC Comet 4s from 1965 to January 1967, one of which they bought in December 1966. This brought the BOAC/KAC co-operation to an end.

Twin Pioneer G-APHY (c/n 508), operated by the Kuwait Oil Company, seen at Doha in 1958.

1945~1967

Above: Hermes 4 OD-ACC G-ALDY (c/n HP.81/25) was one of two Handley Page H.P. 81 Hermes 4s leased from Skyways Ltd. for a three month period from 3rd July 1955.

Left:
After service with the airline, Douglas C-47A OD-AAN (c/n 9894) was sold in the U.S.A. becoming N219F in 1965.

Below: Shot at Blackbush in 1956, the single MEA-operated Bristol 170 Freighter Mk.31E OD-ACM (c/n 13072) 'Doha'. She was flown from December 1955 to May 1958.

1945~1967

Avro York C.1 G-AHFD (c/n 1307), ex-BSAAC and BOAC, taken at Beirut in 1957 wearing the full livery of Middle East Airlines.

Middle East Airlines (MEA) was founded in Beirut on the 31st May 1945 by Lebanese interests who later signed an agreement with BOAC on the 28th August to supply technical assistance and aircraft. On the 22nd November, three DH.89A Rapides arrived from England and began scheduled services in January 1946 from Beirut-Nicosia and Beirut-Aleppo, Syria. Later in the year, services were operated to Baghdad, Cairo and Damascus with the addition of three DC-3s.

In August 1949, BOAC was ousted by Pan American who exchanged three DC-3s for 36% of MEA shares. During the 1950's, however, MEA needed modern equipment to compete with local airlines, but Pan American was reluctant to invest any capital. MEA therefore bought

BOAC Comet 4 G-APDA (c/n 6401) was leased to MEA from November 1960 to March 1961. Here the aircraft is seen at Heathrow Airport during February 1961.

1945~1967

Vickers Viscount V.754D OD-ACX (c/n 245) basks in the sunshine at Beirut in 1962.

out the Pan American shares in early 1955 and approached BOAC once again.

BOAC bought 48.43% of MEA in April 1955 and ordered eight new Viscounts for delivery during 1957, as well as signing a two year lease agreement with Hunting-Clan for three Viscount V.732s. Hunting-Clan was a BOAC partner in the Mideast Aircraft Service Company (MASCO) which was formed in Beirut in 1955 to repair and maintain aircraft, including Viscounts. The three Viscounts were delayed, however, so two

Hermes 4s were leased from Skyways of London for three months as an interim measure, operating from Beirut to Baghdad, Cairo and the Persian Gulf in July 1955. The Hunting Viscounts arrived in October and operated from Beirut to Baghdad, Bahrain, Cairo and Dhahran, and in November from Beirut-Athens-Rome.

By 1956 the popular Viscounts also operated to Ankara, Istanbul, Jeddah, Kuwait, London, Paris, Teheran, Vienna and Zurich, but in September 1957 they were replaced by MEA's

Two Viscount V.754Ds OD-ACW (c/n 242) and OD-ACX (c/n 245), sit in company with an Air Liban Caravelle at Beirut in 1962.

1945~1967

MEA/Air Liban Douglas DC-4 OD-ACI (c/n 10483) seen at Heathrow in 1959.

own Viscount 745Ds. MEA had a single Bristol Freighter, and bought three Avro York freighters from Skyways in June 1957 to operate scheduled cargo routes between the Persian Gulf and Europe. However this venture generated heavy losses and, by March 1959, the remaining two Yorks were withdrawn and sold, leaving MEA with seven Viscounts and four DC-3s.

MEA ordered four new Comet 4C jets, recommended by BOAC who acted as guar-

antor. They signed a joint pool agreement on the London-Beirut-Persian Gulf route, with MEA using BOAC Comet 4s from November 1960 until March 1961 when their Comet 4Cs arrived. In the summer of 1961, BOAC sold its 48.43% shareholding to Sheikh Najib Alamuddin, Chairman and MD of MEA. The pool agreement was enlarged in 1963/64 when Kuwait Airways joined, but they left after two years. The BOAC/MEA agreement continued until 1967.

De Havilland DH.106 Comet 4C OD-ADS (c/n 6448) is serviced at Asgul, Beirut in 1962.

1945~1958

The first of three Vickers-Armstrong V. 644 Viking type 1Bs (c/n 230) YI-ABP 'Al Mahfouthah' was delivered to Iraqi Airways in Baghdad during October 1947 and operated successfully for many years. It is believed to have been withdrawn in 1955.

The Government owned Iraqi State Railways formed Iraqi Airways Ltd. in December 1945 with technical assistance and staff seconded from BOAC. They acquired five DH.89A Rapides to inaugurate domestic services on 29th January 1946 from Baghdad-Basra, a port on an outlet to the Persian Gulf, taking 2hrs 15mins for the 278 miles/447 kms. It was later extended from Basra to Kuwait, a further 87 miles/140 kms, taking 50mins, and also from Baghdad-Mosul.

From December 1946 to July 1947, four Douglas DC-3s were leased from BOAC/BEA for international services from Baghdad-Jerusalem-Cairo, Baghdad-Damascus-Beirut and Baghdad-Tehran. The Rapides were then replaced with three de Havilland DH.104 Dove 1s in late 1947 and the DC-3s were replaced with three Vickers Viking 1Bs delivered in October and December 1947 and January 1948, both types ordered through BOAC.

The popularity of air travel increased and routes were extended from Beirut-Cyprus-Athens, Kuwait-Bahrain and Mosul-Aleppo. A route to London was established with the Vikings and in 1953 another Viking joined the fleet.

BOAC's seconded staff were gradually reduced and replaced by Iraqi staff who had been trained in the UK by BOAC and Air Services Training Ltd. at Aldermaston.

Three Viscounts were delivered in 1955 to replace the Vikings on international routes and, by April 1956, Viscounts operated to Europe from Baghdad-Istanbul-Vienna-London. Because of their superior performance, two more Viscounts were added in 1957 and 1958 and a new route operated from Baghdad-Bahrain-Karachi-Bombay.

BOAC contracts with Iraqi Airways continued until at least 1958 but no record has been found of BOAC's involvement after this date.

Vickers-Armstrong V.735 Viscount YI-ACL (c/n 68) 'Sindbad' at Bahrain in 1960.

1958~1974

De Havilland DH.114 Heron Mk.2 TC-HIZ (c/n14063) of Devlet Hava Yollari-Turkish Airlines.

In May 1933, the Turkish Government formed Devlet Hava Yollari with their first service operating from Istanbul to Ankara using de Havilland DH.89 Dragon Rapides. The airline's name was later changed to Turk Hava Yollari (THY) on 1st March 1956 and, in 1958, BOAC loaned the airline £1.5 million to buy five Vickers Viscounts.

BOAC bought 6% of the airline's shares in 1959 for £500,000 when THY were operating twenty-one Dakotas, seven Herons and four Viscounts on regional and international routes in the Middle East. Five Fairchild F-227s were also ordered and delivered in 1961.

Services to Western Europe were operated with Viscounts from Istanbul-Athens-Rome and Istanbul-Vienna-Frankfurt-Brussels. Viscounts were also used on Middle East services from Istanbul-Ankara-Adana-Beirut and Istanbul-Ankara-Tel Aviv, and in 1961/62, services were also extended to London. Fairchild F-227s operated the Istanbul-Izmir-Athens route as well as internal services with the Herons and Dakotas.

Jets were introduced in 1967 when a DC-9-14 was leased from Douglas which operated in Europe and replaced the Viscount. Ten Douglas DC-9-32s were eventually delivered and in 1970 inaugurated a route from Istanbul to London. Passenger traffic increased

Left:
THY operated up to twenty-seven Douglas DC-3s at one time or another on routes throughout the Middle East and on a network of internal services.

Douglas C-47A Dakota TC-YOL (c/n 12060) is seen at Gatwick in the 1960s.

1958~1974

Five Fairchild FH-227s were bought new and were mainly used on internal routes from July 1960 to December 1972. At Ankara on 8th November 1968, TC-KOZ (c/n 87) awaits passengers. The aircraft was sold to Fokker Aircraft in December 1972.

Vickers-Armstrong V.794D Viscount (c/n 246) TC-SEC at Istanbul in April 1971. One of five operated by THY from 1958-1971, it was sold to the Turkish Air Force after Douglas DC-9s were delivered.

Douglas DC-9-14 (c/n 47048) was delivered new to Continental as N8964 in July 1966 but returned to the manufacturer in July 1967. A month later it was leased to THY until March 1973. TC-JAA was their first DC-9, 'Topkapi', seen at Zurich on the 31st March 1968.

and over one million passengers were carried in 1970, rising to two million in 1972. Orders were placed for three Douglas DC-10s to be delivered from 1972 and five Fokker F-28s to be delivered in 1973.

The 6% shares held by BOAC were transferred to British Airways in April 1974, and were reported as sold by British Airways in 1977.

Gallery 1940~1974

Above: *Short Scion VQ-PAB of Palestine Air Transport Ltd. BOAC had 3,050 PAL shares.*

Left:
Indian Trans-Continental Airways (ITCA) was formed on 21st June 1933 by Imperial Airways (24%), the Indian Government (51%) and Indian National Airways (25%) and operated Karachi to Singapore with two Armstrong Whitworth XVs. Photo of VT-AEF (c/n A.W. 740) 'Arethusa'.

Bottom: *Ex-BOAC Handley Page Hermes 4 G-ALDL (c/n HP81/13) now serving as VP-BBP with Bahamas Airways of Nassau in October 1960.*

Gallery 1940~1974

Above: Skyways operated freight services on behalf of BOAC from London-Singapore and London-Hong Kong beginning in November 1954 and lasting until April 1962, when BOAC introduced Boeing 707s to the Far East with larger freight holds and promptly made the Hermes aircraft redundant. This aircraft is ex-BOAC Handley Page Hermes 4 G-ALDY (c/n HP. 81/25) seen at Paya Lebar Singapore in April 1958. After retirement of the Hermes in July 1960, Skyways replaced the aircraft with a number of ex-BOAC 749A Lockheed Constellations also used as freighters.

Below: Rhodesia and Nyasaland Airways Ltd. (R.A.N.A.) was formed on 12th October 1933 with capital of £25,000. The Beit Railway Trust Ltd held 13,000 shares, Imperial Airways (Africa) had 8,000 shares and the previous shareholders of the Rhodesian Aviation Company with 2,477 shares. Seen here in 1938 from left to right are three de Havilland DH.89 Dragon Rapides, a DH.90 Dragonfly and a DH.85 Leopard Moth standing smartly in-line.

BIBLIOGRAPHY

BOOKS

Allen, Eric, *Airliners in Australian Service, Vol 1* (1995), (Aerospace Publications, Australia)

Allen, Eric, *Airliners in Australian Service, Vol 2* (1996), (Aerospace Publications, Australia)

Andrews, C.F. *Vickers Aircraft since 1908* (Putnam, 1967)

Barker, Dudley. *Merchant Airman - The Air Ministry Account of British Civil Aviation 1939-1944* (HMSO 1946, England)

Barnes, C.H. *Bristol Aircraft since 1910* (Putnam, 1964)

Barnes, C.H. *Handley Page Aircraft since 1907*. Putnam,1976.

Barnes, C.H. *Shorts Aircraft since 1900* (Putnam, 1967)

Barnes, F.G. & Church,R.J. *British Aerospace 748* (Air Britain, 1986)

Bowers, Peter M. *Boeing Aircraft since 1916* (Putnam, 1966)

Bray, Winston *The History of BOAC 1939-1974* (Wessex Press, England [Circa 1985])

Brooks, Peter W. *The World's Airliners* (Putnam, 1962)

Brown, Don L. *Miles Aircraft since 1925* (Putnam, 1970)

Cowell, J. Graham, *de Havilland Heron* (England, 1983)

Curtis, Lettice, *The Forgotten Pilots (of the ATA)* (Nelson & Saunders, England, 1985)

Davies, R.E.G. *Airlines of Asia since 1920* (Putnam, 1997)

Davies, R.E.G. *Airlines of Latin America since 1919* (Putnam, 1984)

Davies, R.E.G. *Airlines of the USA since 1914* (Putnam, 1972)

Davies, R.E.G. *A History of the World's Airlines* (OUP, 1964)

Davis, Peter J. *East African-An Airline Story* (Runnymede, England)

Driscoll, Ian H. *Airline* (Shortland, Auckland, N.Z., 1979)

Driscoll, Ian H. *Flightpath South Pacific* (Whitcombe and Tombs, Christchurch, N.Z., 1972)

Duval, G.R. *British Flying Boats & Amphibians 1909-52* (Putnam, 1966)

Eather, Charles (Chic) Edward James, *Syd's Pirates (Story of C.P.A.)* (Durnmount, Sydney, Australia, 1983)

Edwards, Sir Ronald. *British Air Transport in the Seventies: Report of the Committee of Inquiry into Civil Air Transport, Cmnd 4018.(H.M.S.O., London, 1969)

Francillon, Rene J. *Lockheed Aircraft since 1913* (Putnam, 1987)

Gradidge, J.M. *The Convairliners Story* (Air Britain, 1997)

Gunston, Bill, *Jane's Aerospace Dictionary* (England,1988)

Hamlin, John F. *The de Havilland Dragon, Rapide Family.* (Air Britain 2003).

Hamlin, John F. *The Oxford, Consul & Envoy File.* (Air Britain 2001).

Hedges, David, *The Eagle Years 1948 - 1968* (The Aviation Hobby Shop, 2001)

Henderson, Scott, *Silent Swift Superb: The Story of the Vickers VC10* (Scoval, 1998)

Henderson, Scott. *Lockheed Constellation.* (Scoval, 2005)

Jackson, A.J. *Avro Aircraft since 1908* (Putnam, 1965)

Jackson, A.J. *British Civil Aircraft 1919-59, Vol 1 & 2* (Putnam, 1959)

Jackson, A.J. *British Civil Aircraft since 1919, Vols 1, 2 & 3* (Putnam, 1973)

Jackson, A.J. *De Havilland since 1909* (Putnam, 1962)

Jamall, Enver, *I Remember (Memories of Civil Aviation on the Sub-Continent 1939-81)* (Enver Jamall, May 1989)

Jane's All the World's Aircraft (Authors include C.G Grey, Leonard Bridgeman and John.W.R.Taylor. Various publishers e.g. Sampson Low)

Jones, A C Merton, *British Independent Airlines since 1946 Volume 1-4* (LAAS & Merseyside Aviation Society, 1977)

Knott, Capt Richard C, *The American Flying Boat* (Conway Maritime Press, London 1970)

Lowe, David, *The Flying-Boat Era* (The Lodestar Press, New Zealand, 1978).

Marson, Peter J. *The Lockheed Series.* (Air Britain 1982).

Marson, Peter J. *The Lockheed Twins.* (Air Britain 2001).

Martin, Bernard, *Viking, Valetta and Varsity* (Air Britain, England, 1975)

McKim, Frank, *The Whispering Giant: The Story of the Bristol Britannia* (Scoval, 2003)

Milberry, Larry, *The Canadair North Star* (Canav Books, Canada, 1982)

Molson, K.M. and Taylor H.A. *Canadian Aircraft since 1909* (Putnam, 1982)

Moore, H.M. *Silver Wings in Pacific Skies, (Story of BCPA)* (Boolarong Publications, Australia, 1993)

Munson, Kenneth, *Pictorial History of BOAC and Imperial Airways* (Ian Allan, 1970)

Pudney, John, *The Seven Skies. A Study of BOAC & its Forerunners since 1919* (Putnam, 1959)

Roadcap, Roy R. *World Airline Record* 1952 (Roy R. Roadcap & Associates, Chicago, USA)

Robertson, Bruce, *Lancaster, The story of a famous Bomber* (Harleyford Publications, England, 1964)

Stackhouse, John, *From the Dawn of Aviation: The Qantas Story 1920~1995* (Focus Publishing, Australia, 1995)

Stackhouse, John, *The Longest Hop, Celebrating 50 years of the Qantas Kangaroo Route 1947-1997* (Focus Publishing, Australia, 1997)

Spragg, C St John, *British Airways* (Thomas Nelson & Sons Ltd, 1938)

Stroud, John, *Airports of the World: 1980* (Putnam, 1980)

Stroud, John, *Annals of British & Commonwealth Air Transport* (Putnam, 1961)

Stroud, John, *European Transport Aircraft since 1910* (Putnam,1966)

Stroud, John, *Passenger Aircraft and their Interiors 1910-2006* (Scoval, 2002)

Tapper, Oliver, *Armstrong Whitworth Aircraft since 1913* (Putnam, 1973)

Tagg, A.E and Wheeler, R.L. *From Sea to Air, the Heritage of Sam Saunders* (Crossprint, 1989)

Taylor, H.A. *Airspeed Aircraft since 1931* (Putnam, 1970)

Todd, T. *Air Transport & Civil Aviation 1944-1945* (Todd Reference Books Ltd, London)

Todd, T. *International Air Transport: 1947* (Todd Reference Books Ltd, London)

Walker, Timothy, *The First Jet Airliner: The Story of the de Havilland Comet* (Scoval, 2000)

Wegg, John, *General Dynamics Aircraft and their Predecessors* (Putnam, 1990)

Young, Gavin, *Beyond Lion Rock. The Story of Cathay Pacific Airways* (Hutchinson, 1988)

GLOSSARY & ABBREVIATIONS

A.A.A. ....Arab Airlines Association Ltd.
A.B.A. ....Aktiebolaget Aerotransport(Swedish Airlines)
A.B.A.M.E.L. ....Associated British Airlines (Middle East) Ltd.
A.I.I. ....Air India International
A.N.A. ....Australian National Airways Pty. Ltd.
A.N.A.C. ....Australian National Airlines Commission
A.N.Z. ....Air New Zealand Ltd.
A.O.A. ....American Overseas Airlines
A.S.G.U.L. ....Aircraft Services Gulf Ltd.
A.T.A. ....Air Transport Auxiliary
A.T.L. ....Aviation Traders (Engineering) Ltd.
A.T.F.E.R.O. ....Atlantic Ferry Organisation
A.W. ....Armstrong Whitworth
B.A. ....British Airways PLC
B.A.A.C ....British Airways Associated Companies
B.A.B. ....British Airways Board
B.A.C. ....British Aircraft Corporation. (became BAe)
B.Ae ....British Aerospace Ltd.
B.A.L. ....British Airways Ltd.
B.A.L.P.A. ....British Air Line Pilots Association
B.A.R.U. ....British Airways Repair Unit
B.C.A. ....British Caribbean Airways
B.C.L. ....BOAC-Cunard Ltd.
B.C.P.A. ....British Commonwealth Pacific Airlines Ltd.
B.E.A. ....British European Airways
B.E.A.C. ....British European Airways Corporation
B.E.F. ....British Expeditionary Forces
B.E.O.L. ....BOAC Engine Overhaul Ltd.
B.G.A. ....British Guiana Airways Ltd.
B.H.A. ....British Honduras Airways
B.I.A. ....British International Airlines
B.K.S. ....Barnby, Keegan and Stevens (Air Transport) Ltd.
B.L.A.A.L ....British Latin American Air Lines Ltd.
B.O.A.C. ....British Overseas Airways Corporation

B.O.A.C-A.C. ....BOAC Associated Companies
B.S.A.A. ....British South American Airways Ltd.
B.S.A.A.C. ....British South American Airways Corporation
B.U.A. ....British United Airways Ltd.
B.W.I.A. ....British West Indian Airways
C.A.A. ....Central African Airways
C.A.A. ....Civil Aviation Authority (U.K.)
C.E.O. ....Chief Executive Officer
C.G.T.A.S. ....Canadian Government Trans-Alantic Air Service
c/n ....Construction number
C.P.A. ....Cathay Pacific Airways
C.P.A.S.................................Canadian Pacific Air Services
C.V. ....Consolidated Vultee (Aircraft Corporation)
D.H. ....De Havilland.(Aeroplane Company England)
D.H.A. ....De Havilland Australia
D.H.C. ....De Havilland Canada
D.H.Y. ....Devlet Hava Yollari (Turkish State Airlines)
E.A.A.C.............................East African Airways Corporation
E.A.M.S. ....Empire Air Mail Scheme
E.C.A. ....Elders Colonial Airways
Etops ....Extended twin (engine) operations
F.A.A. ....Federal Aviation Administration (U.S.A)
G.A. ....Gulf Aviation Company Ltd.
H.F. ......High Frequency (long-range radio communications)
H.K.A. ....Hong Kong Airways Ltd.
H.R.H. ....His Royal Highness/Her Royal Highness
H.S. ....Hawker Siddeley Ltd.
I.A.L. ....Imperial Airways Ltd.
I.T.C.A. ....Indian Trans-Continental Airways
K.A.C...Kuwait Airways Corporation
K.L.M. ....Koninklijke Luchtvaart Maatschappij N.V.
....(Royal Dutch Airlines)
K.N.A. ....Kuwait National Airways Ltd.
K.O.C. ....Kuwait Oil Company Ltd.

GLOSSARY & ABBREVIATIONS

L.A.I.	Linee Aeree Italiane
L.I.A.T.	Leeward Island Air Transport Services Ltd.
L.O.T.	Polskie Linje Lotnicze. (Polish Air Lines)
M.A.L.	Malayan Airways Ltd.
M.A.P.	Ministry of Aircraft Production
M.A.S.	Malaysian Airline System
M.A.S.C.O.	Mideast Aircraft Service Company
M.E.A.	Middle East Airlines
M.O.T.A.T.	Museum of Transport and Technology, Auckland
M.S.A.	Malaysia Singapore Airlines
N.A.C.	National Air Communications
N.Z.N.A.C.	New Zealand National Airways Corporation
P.A.A.	Pan American Airways
P.C.F.	Passenger-Cum-Freighter
P.E.R.A.	Propeller and Engine Repair Auxiliary
P.I.A.	Pakistan International Airlines
P.L.O.	Palestine Liberation Organisation
P.N.G.	Papua New Guinea
Q.A.N.T.A.S.	Queensland and Northern Territory Aerial Service Ltd.
Q.E.A.	Qantas Empire Airways Ltd.
R.A.F.	Royal Air Force
R.A.N.A.	Rhodesia & Nyasaland Airways Ltd.
R.F.S.	Return Ferry Service
R.M.A.	Royal Mail Aircraft
R.N.	Royal Navy
R.N.Z.A.F.	Royal New Zealand Air Force
S.R.A.S.	Southern Rhodesian Air Services
S.A.A.	South African Airways
S.A.A.F.	South African Air Force
S.A.B.E.N.A.	Société Anonyme Belge d'Exploitation de la Navigation Aérienne
S.A.S.	Scandinavian Airlines Systems
S.E.P.	Smiths Electronic Pilot
S.I.A.	Singapore Airlines
S.K.A.T.	Seychelles-Kilimanjaro Air Transport
S.L.A.	Sierra Leone Airways Ltd.
s/n	serial number
S.P.A.T.C.	South Pacific Air Transport Council
S.T.O.L.	Short take-off and landing
T.A.A.	Trans Australia Airlines
T.A.C.A.	Transportes Aéreas Centro-Americanos
T.C.A.	Trans-Canada Air Lines
T.E.A.L.	Tasman Empire Airways Limited
T.H.Y.	Turk Hava Yollari (Turkish Airlines)
U.S.A.F.	United States Air Force
VE Day	8th May 1945
VIASA	Vías Internacionales Aéreas, S.A.
V.I.P.	Very Important Person
VJ Day	15th August 1945
W.A.A.C.	West African Airways Corporation
WWII	World War Two. (1939-1945)

APPENDICES

BOAC AIRCRAFT CLASSES AND NAMES

Atalanta class .... Armstrong Whitworth A.W. 15 Atalanta

Argonaut class .... Canadair C-4

Bermuda class .... Short S.25 Sandringham 7

B names .... Boeing 314A

B names .... Lockheed Constellation

C class .... Short S.23 Empire Boat

C class .... Short S.30 Empire Boat

C class .... Short S.33 Empire Boat

C names... Boeing 377 Stratocruiser

Diana class .... de Haviland DH.86 Express

Ensign class .... Armstrong Whitworth A.W.27 Ensign

Frobisher class......................... de Havilland DH.91 Albatross

F names .... Handley Page HP. 70 Halton

G class .... Short S.26

Hannibal class .... Handley Page HP.42 (HP42E Eastern)

Heracles class .... Handley Page HP.45 (HP42W Western)

Hythe class .... converted Short S.25 Sunderland III

Hermes class .... Handley Page HP.81 Hermes

Junkers class .... Junkers JU52/3m

King class................................. de Havilland DH.95 Flamingo

Lockheed class .... Lockheed 10A Electra

Lockheed class .... Lockheed 14 Super Electra

Lockheed class .... Lockheed 18 Lodestar

M names ....Avro 685 York

Maia .... Short-Mayo Composite S.21 (lower component)

Mercury ...... Short-Mayo Composite S.20 (upper component)

N names .... Avro 691 Lancastrian

Plymouth class .... Short S.25 Sandringham 5

St. Louis .... Curtiss Wright CW-20 ....

S names .... Short S.45 Solent 2

Sandringham class .... Short S.25 Sandringham 1

Star .... ex-BSAA aircraft

Wulf .... Focke-Wulf Fw200A-02 Condor

BOAC SERVICE CLASSES:

Bahamian .... First-class (New York-Nassau)

Beaver .... Tourist (UK-Canada)

Bermudian .... Tourist (New York-Bermuda)

Coronet .... Tourist

Jamaican .... Tourist (New York-Jamaica)

Majestic .... First-class (Africa, Asia & Australia)

Mayflower .... Tourist. (UK-USA)

Monarch .... First-class (Trans-atlantic)

CHAIRMEN OF BOAC:

Sir John Reith .... 24 November 1939 - 5 March 1940

Hon. Clive Pearson .... 6 March 1940 - 24 March 1943

Sir Harold Howitt .... 24 March 1943 - 25 May 1943

Viscount Knollys .... 26 May 1943 - 30 June 1947

Sir Harold Hartley .... 1 July 1947 - 30 June 1949

Sir Miles Thomas........................ 1 July 1949 - 30 April 1956

Sir Gerard d'Erlanger .... 1 May 1956 - 28 July 1960

Sir Matthew Slattery ...... 29 July 1960 - 31 December 1968

Sir Charles Hardie .... 1 January 1969 - 31 December 1970

Sir Keith Granville .... 1 January 1971 - 31 August 1972

Sir Ross Stainton .... 1 September 1972 - 31 March 1974

SYMBOLIC ROUTE NAMES:

Coral .... Auckland-Suva-Samoa-Aitutaki-Papeete (TEAL)

Dragon .... UK-Hong Kong (BOAC)

Hibiscus .... Auckland-Nadi (TEAL)

Horseshoe .... South Africa-Egypt-Australia (BOAC/Qantas)

Kangaroo.................................. UK-Australia (BOAC/Qantas)

Southern Cross .... Australia-Pacific-USA (Qantas)

Speedman .... UK-Argentina (BSAAC)

Springbok .... UK-South Africa (BOAC/SAA)

Tiger .... UK-India (BOAC)

Wallaby .... Australia-South Africa (Qantas)

INDEX

INDEX

ANNUAL REPORTS

British Airways PLC.
British European Airways Corporation
British Overseas Airways Corporation
Civil Aviation, Dept. of Civil Aviation, Air Ministry. H.M.S.O.
Civil Aviation, Ministry of Civil Aviation. H.M.S.O.

CIVIL AIRCRAFT REGISTERS

African Register 1981 (Air Britain)
Australia, New Zealand & SW Pacific Islands Civil Aircraft
        Registers: 1977 (Air Britain)
Central America & the Caribbean Civil Aircraft Registers:
        1978 (Air Britain)
South-East Asia Civil Aircraft Registers: 1979 (Air Britain)
Southern Europe & the Middle East Civil Aircraft Registers:
        1980 (Air Britain)
British Civil Aircraft Registers 1919-1978. John Appleton and
        Ian G. Cave (Midland Counties, 1978)
International Registers of Civil Aircraft: 1963-1977 (Bureau
        Veritas, CAA, and Registro Aeronautico Italiano)

PRODUCTION LISTS

Jet Airliner Production. John Roach & Tony Eastwood (The
        Aviation Hobby Shop)
Piston Engine Airliner Production. John Roach & Tony
        Eastwood (The Aviation Hobby Shop)
Turbo Prop Airliner Production. John Roach & Tony Eastwood
        (The Aviation Hobby Shop)
More than half a Century of Soviet Transports. Peter
        Hillman, Stuart Jessup, Adrian Morris, Tony Morris,
        Guus Ottenhof Michael Roch (4th Edition, 2003)

PERIODICALS

ABC World Airways Guide (Dunstable, England)
Aeroplane Monthly and The Aeroplane (London)
Air BP (British Petroleum Co Ltd, London)
Air Pictorial (St Leonards on Sea, England)
*British Airways News Letter / British Overseas Airways News
        Letter / BOAC Review / BOAC Newsletter* (England)
De Havilland Gazette (Hatfield, England)
Esso Air World (New York)
Flight also *Flight International* (London)
Propliner (England)
Whites Aviation Monthly (Wellington, New Zealand)